P9-CQP-288

1000 BOOKS READING CHALLENGE

Sticker Book, Activities, and App Companion

Beanstack Badge Books
2021 - 2022

beanstack.com

This book belongs to:

How To Use This Book

**This Badge Book works hand-in-hand with
the Beanstack Tracker App.**

For everyone:
Download the mobile app
for Android or iPhone.

OR

For library or school users:
Visit your Beanstack site.
Not sure what that is? Go to:
beanstack.com/find-a-site

**The app is the easy way to make sure you
get credit for every book you read.**

1. The app will guide you straight to your free account.
   *If you bought this book yourself, you can scan the book's barcode
   when prompted to subscribe.

2. Under Discover/Challenges, find the 1000
   Books reading challenge and tap to register.

3. Tap the log button ("+" button in the
   mobile app) to start logging your reading
   and activities.

4. You can scan the barcode of any book for
   instant logging. No typing needed.

This book also comes with
LOTS OF STICKERS

**Numbered stickers
track your progress
towards your
1000 Books goal.**

**Star stickers match
the family activities
in the book.**

If your child is still too small to handle the stickers, you have our permission to peel
and stick them yourself. Researchers agree: Stickers are fun at any age.

Now, what should you count towards your 1000 Books goal?

EVERYTHING!

- Board books
- Picture books
- Wordless books

- Chapter Books
- Comic books
- Baby books

- Kids Magazines
- Articles
- Poems

Need more ideas? Flip to the back of this book for a handy list of 1000 quality titles, sorted by interest and age range.

And the big question: "Do re-reads count each time?"

✔ YES, of course!

Any time you sit and read with you child, it counts— **the experience is what matters most.**

TIPS

The badges you earn in the app may not always match the stickers in the book. It depends on your library, school, or company.

The activities are just for fun. Do as many or as few as you like!

Questions? Visit badgebook.com/getstarted, or check with your library or school. It only takes a minute or two to be up and reading!

Feeling a little daunted by the number 1000? Turn the page and let us **pump you up.**

WHY 1000 BOOKS?

One *thousand* books? That seems like way too many, right? Not at all. **You got this.** Even one book a day for three years will get you to 1095, well past your goal. It doesn't matter if your child is three, or just three months—there's no better time to start than now!

So why read 1000 books together? You've probably heard reasons like these:

 Big Vocabulary. Children who read 20 minutes a day take in 1.8 million words per year.[1]

 Big Brain. Reading aloud boosts cognitive development[2] at an age when your child's brain is growing rapidly.

 Better Grades. Kids whose grown-ups read to them have strong vocabularies, write well, and do well overall in school.[3]

And yes, those things are absolutely true!

But that's not all.

 "Words mean more than what is set down on paper. It takes the human voice to infuse them with deeper meaning."

– MAYA ANGELOU

The benefits of reading go way beyond school prep:

1 **Reading bonds you.** Cuddling close while immersed in a book is a uniquely powerful connection.

2 **Reading calms kids down.** Just six minutes can reduce stress levels by 68%.[4]

3 **Reading builds social and emotional skills.** Books give kids language to express "big feelings," and can even improve empathy for others.[5]

4 **Reading kids are happier kids.** Children most engaged with reading are three times as likely to have high levels of mental well-being.[6]

5 **Reading makes you a role model.** Show your own love of books! Kids whose parents are frequent readers become frequent readers themselves.[7]

6 **Reading sparks creativity and imagination.** Books are windows that open to new worlds. They inspire creativity and stretch kids' notions of what is possible.

Take that motivation, open one book, and get started. **And remember, 1000 is just a number.** Whether you read 200 or 2000 books, your child will treasure those minutes together. The goal is to work reading aloud into your regular routine, and let the magic of stories do the rest.

―――――

See the last page of this book for references and further reading.

Draw Yourself Here

(For very little readers, trace a hand here)

OUR FAMILY READING PLEDGE

⭐ We are _____
(Name)

⭐ and _____
(Name)

⭐ Our hometown is _____

_____.

⭐ We like books about _____

_____.

We hereby pledge to read together and share our love of great books!

OFFICIAL SIGNATURES

1000 BOOKS

Reading Challenge

Turn the page
to get your
sign-up sticker!

OUR GOALS

To Read: _____ Books Every Week

To Read Daily:

☐ 20 Minutes   ☐ 30 Minutes

☐ 60 Minutes   ☐ _____ Minutes

A Book We're Excited About Reading:

_____

_____

_____

100
Way to go!
Put your
sticker here.

80

90

70

60

20

10

40

30

50

REMEMBER:
Log reading through
Beanstack to track
your progress and
unlock the stickers!

Date completed: _____

Favorite read: _____

Sign-Up Badge

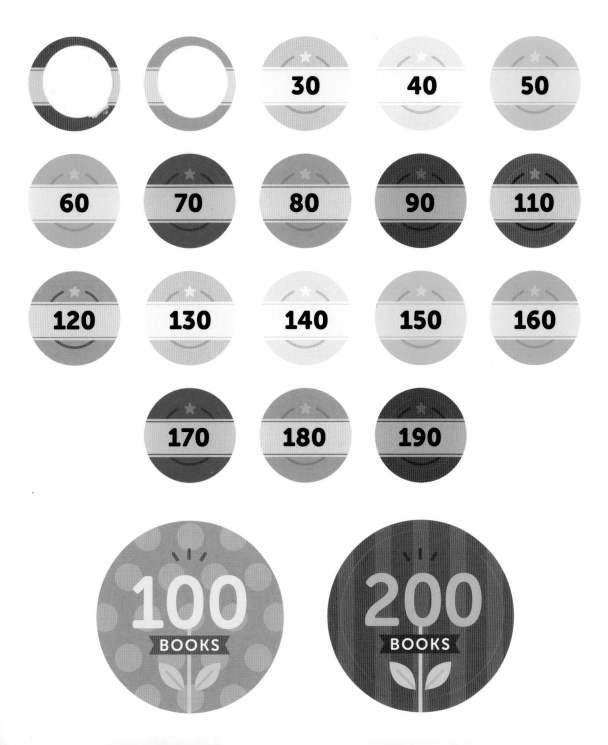

110

120

130

140

150

160

170

180

190

Flowers

200
Stick it to me!
Put your
sticker here.

REMEMBER:
Log reading through
Beanstack to track
your progress and
unlock the stickers!

Date completed: _____

Favorite read: _____
_____

210

220

230

240

250

260

300
You da champ!
Put your
sticker here.

290

280

270

REMEMBER:
Log reading through
Beanstack to track
your progress and
unlock the stickers!

Date completed: _____

Favorite read: _____

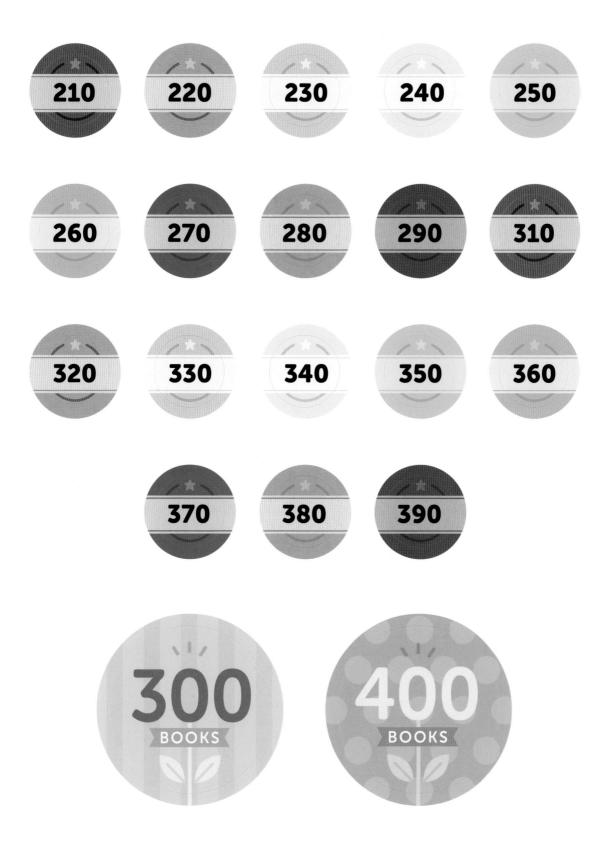

Fresh Produce

310
320
330
340
350

360
370
380
390

400
Top notch-effort!
Put your
sticker here.

REMEMBER:
Log reading through
Beanstack to track
your progress and
unlock the stickers!

Date completed: _____

Favorite read: _____

410 420
430 440 450
460 470 480 490

500
Job well done!
Put your
sticker here.

REMEMBER:
Log reading through
Beanstack to track
your progress and
unlock the stickers!

Date completed: _____

Favorite read: _____

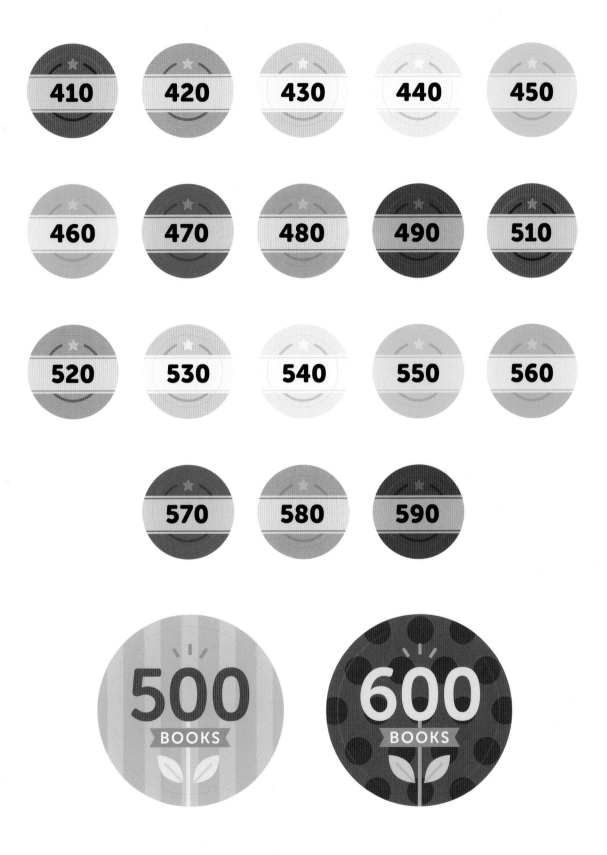

YOU'RE HALFWAY!
HIGHLIGHTS AND FAVORITES

📖 Book We Read More Than Once: _____

_____

😝 A Book That Made Us Laugh: _____

_____

👍 Bravest Character: _____

_____

🎨 Book With the Most Interesting Illustrations:

_____

_____

🗺️ Most Unusual Place We Read a Book: _____

_____

JUST FOR FUN!

Read a book with a friend!

Check the Beanstack app to fill in your stats so far:

Total Minutes Read:

Number of Reading Sessions:

Most Pages in a Session:

Longest Reading Streak:

600
Most impressive!
Put your
sticker here.

REMEMBER:
Log reading through
Beanstack to track
your progress and
unlock the stickers!

Date completed: _____

Favorite read: _____

700
Splendid!
Put your
sticker here.

680

690

660

670

650

640

620

610

630

REMEMBER:
Log reading through
Beanstack to track
your progress and
unlock the stickers!

Date completed: _____

Favorite read: _____

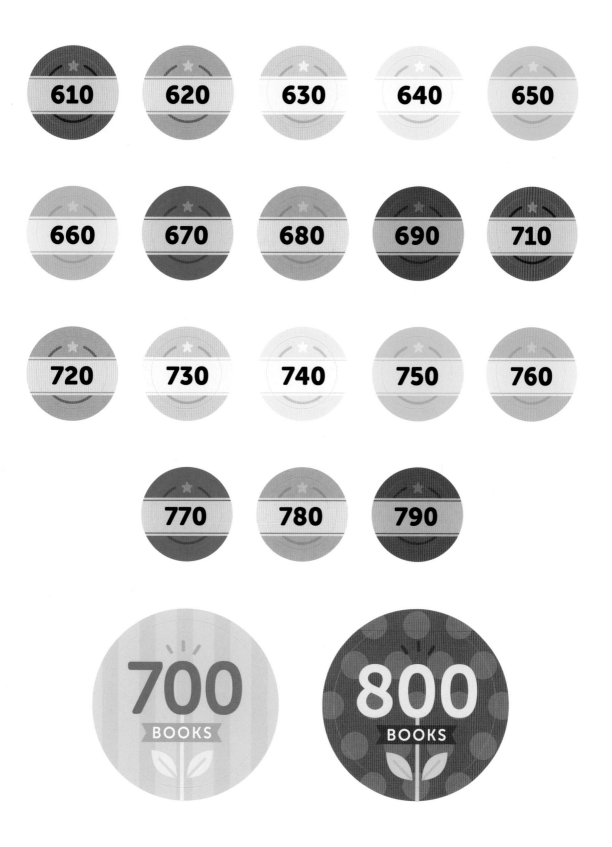

800
You got moxie, kid!
Put your sticker here.

790

780

770

760

750

740

730

720

710

REMEMBER:
Log reading through
Beanstack to track
your progress and
unlock the stickers!

Date completed: _____

Favorite read: _____

850
840
860
830
870
820
880
810
890

900
You go,
power reader!
Put your
sticker here.

REMEMBER:

Log reading through
Beanstack to track
your progress and
unlock the stickers!

Date completed: _____

Favorite read: _____

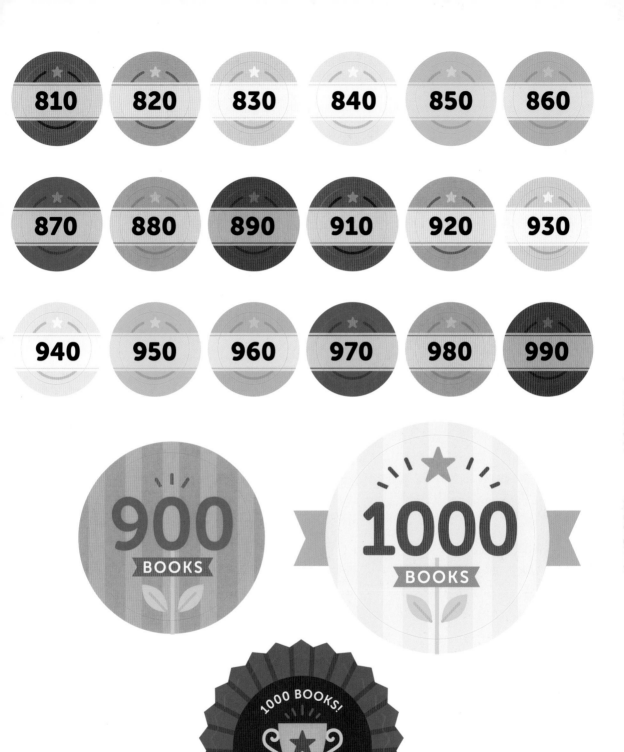

Challenge
Certificate of Completion

1000
Stupendous achievement! Put your sticker here.

940

930

950

920

960

910

970

980

990

YAY!

REMEMBER:
Log reading through Beanstack to track your progress and unlock the stickers!

Date completed: _____

Favorite read: _____

YOU DID IT!
FINAL HIGHLIGHTS AND FAVORITES

📖 Book We'd Recommend to Our Friends:

_____

🌍 A New Place We Read About: _____

_____

😝 Silliest Character: _____

_____

📕 Best Book Cover: _____

_____

👤 Someone New Who Read with Us: _____

_____

_____

☀️ JUST FOR FUN! ☀️

Build a fort you can read inside!

Check the Beanstack app to fill in your final stats:

Total Minutes Read:

Number of Reading Sessions:

Most Pages in a Session:

Longest Reading Streak:

— CERTIFICATE OF —
COMPLETION

Put your
blue ribbon
sticker here!

AWARDED TO:

Names: _____

Date: _____

Number of Badges Earned: _____

Signatures: _____

_____

ACTIVITIES

GET OUT AND READ

Don't limit your read-alouds to the bedroom or the couch! Building a habit of reading means showing your child that books are trusty companions for just about anyplace. Challenge yourselves to log some read-aloud time outside the house.

Great moments to pull out a book:
- At the playground during a snack break
- On the bus (or at the bus stop)
- In the doctor's or dentist's waiting room
- Up on the roof (if your building allows)
- On a playdate
- At a restaurant before the food arrives
- Before karate or dance class
- In the sunshine of your own backyard

TIPS

Stash a book in your bag ahead of time, so you don't have to think of it in the moment when you're wrangling everyone out the door. Books with multiple stories or sections go a lot farther, and don't have to be swapped out after every trip. Try:

1. *Frog and Toad* by Arnold Lobel (Ages 2-4)
2. *Ling and Ting* series by Grace Lin (Ages 3-5)
3. *Little Kids First Big Book of Why* by National Geographic (Ages 2-5)

READ
SOMEWHERE NEW

COOK
WITH BOOKS

WACKY
QUESTIONS

YOUNG
SHERLOCK

SINGING
WITH BOOKS

TOO
MANY BOOKS

PLAYING
WITH BOOKS

READING
PARTY

Use the blanks on this page to note three new places you've read together!

1

2

3

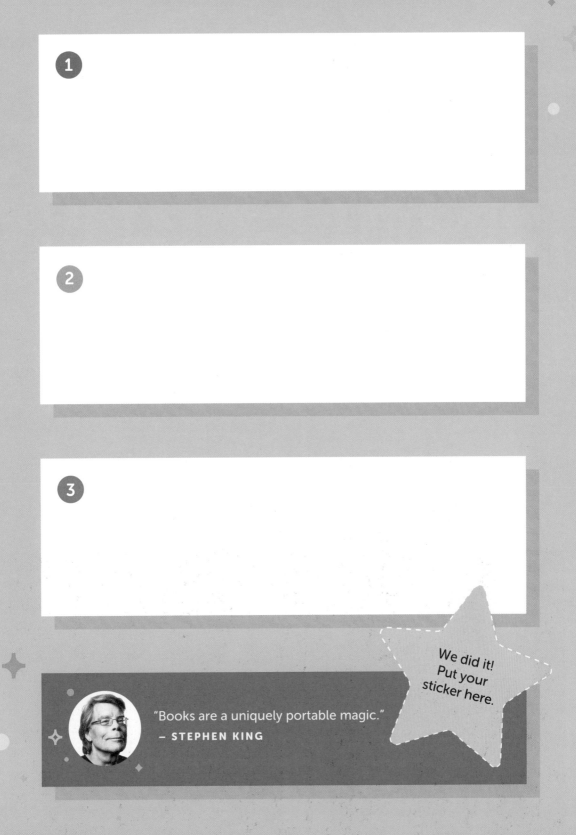

"Books are a uniquely portable magic."
— STEPHEN KING

We did it!
Put your
sticker here.

Read A:
WORDLESS PICTURE BOOK

If you're looking for beautiful, expressive artwork, wordless titles often feature the industry's best illustrators at the top of their game. It's no coincidence that these books win the Caldecott Award with some frequency.

A bonus of wordless books is that they often match a wider range of ages—siblings from toddlers to elementary age can all enjoy the same story together. Start by describing the pictures and narrating the story yourself, and then (if your child is old enough) switch to taking turns, with them narrating some pages. It's engaging and builds their expository language skills.

Here are some wordless titles with wonderful illustrations to get you started. Your librarian can help you find others!

1. *Lion and the Mouse* by Jerry Pinkney (Ages 2-6)
2. *Have You Seen My Duckling* by Nancy Tafuri (Ages 0-4)
3. *Door* by JiHyeon Lee (Ages 2-6)
4. *Fly!* by Mark Teague (Ages 1-4)

COOK WITH BOOKS

Take your reading into the kitchen, and let your child help you create something fun and delicious. Connecting reading to a family activity like cooking brings books to life in a very real, tangible way. Plus, it's a perfect method to introduce some new menu items, or dishes from other cultures—kids are bound to try it if they've helped make it.

Here are some picture books with kid-friendly recipes to get you started. Your librarian can help you find others!

1 *Bee-bim Bop!* by Linda Sue Park

2 *Peeny Butter Fudge* by Toni Morrison

3 *Bilal Cooks Daal* by Aisha Saieed

4 *Mr. Cookie Baker* by Monica Wellington

Rate the Recipe

We made: _____

_____

_____

From the book: _____

_____

_____

Rating: ☓☓   ☹   😐   ☺   😊

We did it!
Put your
sticker here.

"One cannot think well if one
has not dined well."

— VIRGINIA WOOLF

3 WACKY
Questions

Ever feel stuck wondering what subjects to hunt for at the library? Try this line with your child: **"If you could ask the wise library owl three wacky questions about the world, what would you want to know?"**

Taking turns suggesting wacky questions can break the ice, start you both laughing, and get your brains bubbling over with ideas. It's an activity that really picks up momentum, as one thought leads to the next. Here are some starters!

- How are donuts made?
- Where does the bathwater go when it spins down the drain?
- Are there kids who fly airplanes?
- Do bees dance?
- How long will your hair get if you don't cut it?
- What's the biggest truck in the world?
- Are there famous women pirates?
- Can trees talk to each other?
- Why is the desert sandy?
- What happens if you eat crayons?

Jot down your child's questions below, and use them to guide your next library or internet searches.

1

2

3

We did it! Put your sticker here.

"The purpose of education...is to create in a person the ability to look at the world for himself, to make his own decisions."

— JAMES A. BALDWIN

YOUNG SHERLOCK HOLMES

Try this "Detective Game" to liven up storytime. Here's how it works:

1. After you read through a spread in a picture book, your child closes their eyes.

2. Then, you ask questions about the scene, like "OK, what color is the rhino's surfboard?" or "What is flying above the building?"

3. The goal is to answer without peeking.

4. Adjust the difficulty level to keep it fun!

This game works wonders if your child's attention is wandering off during a story, or if they are getting excitable just when you're trying to calm things down before bed.

Prepare to be amazed at how much kids can recall! They truly get immersed in each tiny element of the scenes on the page.

PRO TIPS

Try this with books kids already know well—
it adds new fun to old favorites.

Play only on some pages to avoid losing
the flow of the story.

Use counting, shape, and color
elements ("How many trucks
were racing?"; "What shape was the
boat's sail?") to gently boost
those early skills.

We did it!
Put your
sticker here.

"Before they read words,
children are reading pictures."
— **DAVID WIESNER**

SINGING WITH BOOKS

Singing is a surefire way to capture your child's attention and enliven your playtime. It doesn't matter what your voice sounds like—your singing is beautiful music to your child's ears. With or without books, singing and musical activities at home can help your child's language development.[1]
Ready to get musical?

Little ones are full of energy! Use movement songs to release some of that before they settle down for a story.
- Try "Head, Shoulders, Knees, and Toes" or "The Hokey Pokey" as a lead-in to storytime. Bonus: They'll benefit from the motor-skill practice and opportunity to express themselves.[2]

Sing songs emphasizing the first sound in a word.
For example, "My name is Keisha, and I like cookies. My name is Benny, and I like bananas..." It's a more lively way to practice pre-reading skills.

Use books as a springboard for singing.
Song books (see next page) are obvious options, but you can sing anything! Nursery rhymes, poetry, or simple picture books will all work.

_____

See the last page of this book for references and further reading.

Here are some picture books with simple singalongs to get you started. Your librarian can help you find others!

1. **Down by the Bay** by Raffi (Ages 0-3)
2. **Head, Shoulders, Knees and Toes...** illustrated by Annie Kubler (Ages 0-3)
3. **Singing in the Rain** illustrated by Tim Hopgood (Ages 4-6)
4. **We're Going on a Lion Hunt** by David Axtell (Ages 2-6)
5. **Old Mikamba Had a Farm** by Rachel Isadora (Ages 3-6)

We did it! Put your sticker here.

"Where words fail, music speaks."
– HANS CHRISTIAN ANDERSEN

Read About:
REAL-LIFE HEROES

"Historical biographies" may seem like a dusty category for preschoolers, but don't overlook this genre. Kids are quick to connect to stories of real people, and knowing those stories are true adds an extra layer of interest for young readers. Plus, biographies follow the "show, don't tell" rule of inspiring kids with real examples, and give kids a powerful opportunity to see themselves reflected in famous role models.

Remember, even if the historical context is above their age level, children can still empathize with the struggles—and celebrate the perseverance— of iconic characters from real life.

These books often come in series; here are some true-hero titles to get you started. Your librarian can help you find others!

1. ***Wilma: My First Wilma Rudolph*** – Little People, Big Dreams series (Ages 1-3)

2. ***The Story of the Wright Brothers*** by Michelle Prater Burke – "The Story of" boardbook series (Ages 2-5)

3. ***I Am Frida Kahlo*** by Brad Meltzer – Ordinary People Change the World series. (Ages 3-6)

4. ***A Boy and a Jaguar*** by Alan Rabinowitz (Ages 3-7)

TOO MANY BOOKS

Let's face it: You *can* have too many books for one shelf or one room. If they're winding up in heaps on the floor, or crammed in a cubby, it's doubly counterproductive: For you, a constant mess to manage, and for your child, an obstacle to pulling out a fun title from the chaos.

Montessori schools often limit their books to a dozen or so rotating titles on display at any one time, with the rest of their library stored away on higher shelves.[1] Here are three other ideas to keep your shelves fresh and welcoming:

1 **The Attic Surprise**
Scoop half your child's books into a box for the attic or closet. Set an email or phone reminder (two months is a good length) for when to swap, and then simply exchange the boxed books for the ones on the shelf.

2 **The Book Box Swap**
Load up a batch of titles your kids are tired of, and drop them off (with permission!) at a playmate's house. If they give a few in return, your child will have a bonanza of books with all kinds of new stories to get into.

———

See the last page of this book for references and further reading.

3 The Giver

Developmental psychologists find that gift-giving provides benefits to kids' emotional growth: building empathy, creating a habit of kindness, and elevating children's sense of well-being.[2] If your child is old enough, hand them a grocery bag and ask them to fill it with books to donate to kids who don't have as many.

These places are usually grateful for donations, especially at the holidays:

• Women's shelters
• Fire departments
• Family homeless shelters
• Group homes

If your child understands where their gifts are going—and why—their generosity may surprise you.

QUICK FIX:
A bedside "book basket" for dropping in finished bedtime stories will dramatically cut down on the books-on-the-floor chaos.

We did it! Put your sticker here.

"A book is not an end in itself. A book is a means of communication."

— ISABEL ALLENDE

PLAYING WITH BOOKS

Books are a natural springboard for imaginative play, and using them at playtime shows children that reading can be lively, exciting, and active. Get things moving with these book-related games:

 Name That Face.
Start with a book about feelings and expressions (try *I'm Silly!* by J. L. Holm, or *How Are You Peeling* by S. Freymann). Make exaggerated faces for different emotions and guess how the other person is feeling.

 Follow the Leader.
Take turns leading each other in movements, sounds, faces, or any combination you like. Kids love a chance to play the boss. Lead in with a book like A. Johnson's *Do Like Kyla.*

 Play the Part.
Pick a favorite story, role-play as the characters, and let the game go wherever it takes you! Improvisational play increases problem-solving, executive function, and coping skills.[1] Duos with distinct personalities—think Pooh and Tigger—are a fun place to start.

See the last page of this book for references and further reading.

We sometimes think of play as taking a break from serious learning. But for children, play is serious learning. It's how they build focus, social skills, and creativity, and it requires a lot of planning and problem solving.

Here are some additional titles to encourage play and creativity in your child. Your librarian can help you find others!

1. *Let's Play!* by Hervé Tullet (Ages 2-4)
2. *I Thought I Saw a Bear!* Illustrated by Lydia Nichols (Ages 0-3)
3. *Where the Wild Things Are* by Maurice Sendak (Ages 3-6)
4. *Harold and the Purple Crayon* by Crockett Johnson (Ages 3-6)
5. *Not a Stick* by Antoinette Portis (Ages 3-6)

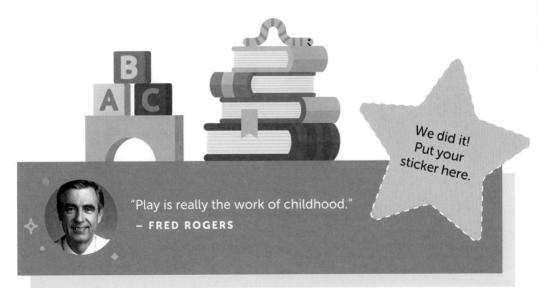

We did it! Put your sticker here.

"Play is really the work of childhood."
— FRED ROGERS

READING PARTY

Put away that tired stereotype of the solitary, lonely reader—after all, for preschoolers, storytime is always a social activity. Reading with friends is a form of sharing—not just sharing the book, but sharing the experience, the interest, and the flight of imagination.

A book party (birthday, playdate, or just-because) is a perfect way to show kids how much their friends love reading, too—and to reinforce their self-image as a proud reader. If your child has an absolute favorite book, plan a party around that specific title. For young preschoolers, though, a broader theme of "We Love Reading" works just fine.

Here are some suggestions for a book-lovers bash:

 SNACKS

- *The Tale of Peter Rabbit* – a tray of baby carrots, snap peas, and other veggies

- *The Very Hungry Caterpillar* – "caterpillar kebabs" of grapes and strawberries

- *Madeline* – French madeleine cookies

- *Dr. Seuss* – "Hop-on-Pop"corn; deviled green eggs with ham

- *Dragons Love Tacos* – tacos, of course!

 ACTIVITIES AND CRAFTS

- Read *Yoko's Paper Cranes* by R. Wells, followed by origami bookmarks.

- Read *The Dot* by P. Reynolds, then try dot paintings.
- Read *Waiting for the Biblioburro* by M. Brown, and play tape-the-book on the burro (like pin-the-tail).
- Read *Journey* by A. Becker, then break out the sidewalk chalk for art.

PARTY FAVORS

- Toy novelty glasses for "reading glasses"
- Gummy "book" worms to take home
- Cloth tote bags for library trips (guests can decorate)

GIFTS

- For birthdays, ask guests to gift a book (used or new).
- For "anytime" parties, ask guests to bring a few used books for a book swap. Everyone can go home with new titles!

We did it!
Put your
sticker here.

"Books always make a room better."
— TANYA BOTEJU

OUR LIBRARY

You've done amazing things, power readers!
Your Beanstack App will show you all the titles you've
read recently—take a look back at those, and fill in some
book titles here to complete your family library.

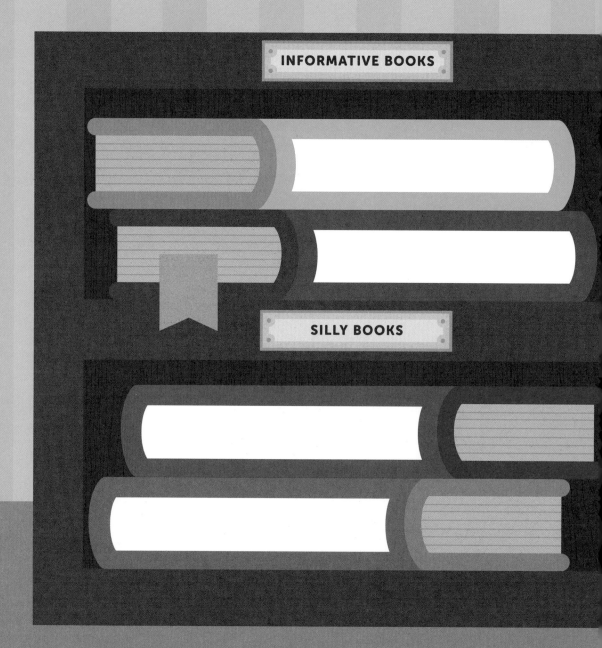

INFORMATIVE BOOKS

SILLY BOOKS

CREATIVE BOOKS

KIND BOOKS

END OF BOOK AWARDS

What an accomplishment!
Put your trophy here.

WAY TO GO!

#1

Names of Reading Superstars

_____

Hail to the Champions!

Guest Book

Show off your reading! Ask your family, teachers, and friends
to check out your Badge Book, sign your guest log,
and leave a comment. You earned it!

Name:

Comments:

Name:

Comments:

Name:

Comments:

Name:

Comments:

Name:

Comments:

Name:

Comments:

Name:

Comments:

Name:

Comments:

Name:

Comments:

BOOKLIST

Looking for something new? We recommend these books for a great range of stories, settings, and characters.

AGES 0-3:

Adventure in the Wide World

- [ ] **Joshua By The Sea** – *Angela Johnson*
- [ ] **The Snowy Day** – *Ezra Jack Keats*
- [ ] **Baby Goes to Market** – *Atinuke*
- [ ] **A Rainbow of My Own** – *Don Freeman*
- [ ] **Baby Day** – *Jane Godwin*
- [ ] **The Wheels on the Tuk Tuk** – *Kabir Sehgal & Surishtha Sehgal*
- [ ] **Babies Around the World** – *Puck*
- [ ] **Around the World in a Bathtub: Bathing All Over the Globe** – *Wade Bradford*
- [ ] **The Three Bears** – *Byron Barton*
- [ ] **Alice's Adventures in Wonderland (Penguin Bedtime Classics)** – *Lewis Carroll*
- [ ] **This is Sadie** – *Sara O'Leary*

Animal Action

- [ ] **Oh No, George!** – *Chris Haughton*
- [ ] **Dinoblock** – *Christopher Franceschelli*
- [ ] **Big Dog and Little Dog Going for a Walk** – *Dav Pilkey*
- [ ] **Have You Seen My Cat?** – *Eric Carle*
- [ ] **Bedtime in the Forest** – *Kazuo Iwamura*
- [ ] **Jump!** – *Tatsuhide Matsuoka*
- [ ] **What Do You Say?** – *Mandy Stanley*
- [ ] **Barnyard Dance!** – *Sandra Boynton*
- [ ] **Jane Foster's Black and White** – *Jane Foster*
- [ ] **Good Dog, Carl** – *Alexandra Day*
- [ ] **Kitten's First Full Moon** – *Kevin Henkes*
- [ ] **Sally at the Farm** – *Stephen Huneck*
- [ ] **I Went Walking** – *Sue Williams*
- [ ] **Little Gorilla** – *Ruth Bornstein*

Classics Old & New

- [ ] **Good Night, Gorilla** – *Peggy Rathmann*

- [ ] **The Wonderful Things You Will Be** – *Emily Winfield Martin*
- [ ] **Grumpy Monkey** – *Suzanne Lang*
- [ ] **If Animals Kissed Good Night** – *Ann Whitford Paul*
- [ ] **Dear Zoo** – *Rod Campbell*
- [ ] **Llama Llama Red Pajama** – *Anna Dewdney*
- [ ] **Five Little Monkeys Jumping on the Bed** – *Eileen Christelow*
- [ ] **Big Red Barn** – *Margaret Wise Brown*
- [ ] **Goodnight Moon** – *Margaret Wise Brown*
- [ ] **Guess How Much I Love You** – *Sam McBratney*
- [ ] **Little Blue Truck** – *Alice Schertle*
- [ ] **Pat the Bunny** – *Dorothy Kunhardt*
- [ ] **Brown Bear, Brown Bear, What Do You See?** – *Bill Martin Jr. & Eric Carle*
- [ ] **The Poky Little Puppy** – *Janette Sebring Lowrey*
- [ ] **The Very Hungry Caterpillar** – *Eric Carle*
- [ ] **Rosie's Walk** – *Pat Hutchins*
- [ ] **Love You Forever** – *Robert Munsch*
- [ ] **The Carrot Seed** – *Ruth Krauss*
- [ ] **The Napping House** – *Audrey Wood*
- [ ] **The Pout-Pout Fish** – *Deborah Diesen*
- [ ] **Chicka Chicka Boom Boom** – *Bill Martin Jr. & John Archambault*

"Reading should not be presented to children as a chore or duty. It should be offered to them as a precious gift."

– KATE DICAMILLO

"My purpose is to create a mirror for the reader to see themselves... so they resonate."

– KADIR NELSON

Who We Are

- [ ] **Everywhere Babies** – *Susan Meyers*
- [ ] **No Matter What** – *Debi Gliori*
- [ ] **The Grouchy Ladybug** – *Eric Carle*
- [ ] **I Love You, Stinky Face** – *Lisa Mccourt*
- [ ] **I Like Me!** – *Nancy Carlson*
- [ ] **You Are Awesome** – *Susann Hoffmann*
- [ ] **It's Okay To Be Different** – *Todd Parr*
- [ ] **Feminist Baby** – *Loryn Brantz*
- [ ] **I am Unstoppable: A Little Book About Amelia Earhart** – *Brad Meltzer*
- [ ] **Baby Astronaut** – *Dr. Laura Gehl*
- [ ] **This Little Trailblazer: A Girl Power Primer** – *Joan Holub*
- [ ] **Dream Big** – *Joyce Wan*
- [ ] **Baby Feminists** – *Libby Babbott-Klein*
- [ ] **ABC for Me: ABC What Can She Be?** – *Sugar Snap Studio & Jessie Ford*
- [ ] **Global Baby Girls** – *The Global Fund for Children*
- [ ] **Dream Big, Little One** – *Vashti Harrison*
- [ ] **The Colors of Us** – *Karen Katz*
- [ ] **Pretty Brown Face** – *Andrea Davis Pinkney*
- [ ] **Cradle M** – *Debby Slier*
- [ ] **Global Babies** – *The Global Fund for Children*

Feelings & Friendship

- [ ] **Roary the Lion Roars Too Loud** – *Ame Dyckman*
- [ ] **You Are Not Small** – *Anna Kang*
- [ ] **Jamberry** – *Bruce Degen*
- [ ] **Penguin and Pinecone: A Friendship Story** – *Salina Yoon*
- [ ] **Bye-Bye Binky** – *Maria van Lieshout*
- [ ] **Go to Bed, Fred** – *Alison Inches*
- [ ] **Someday** – *Alison McGhee*

- [ ] **That's Not Mine** – *Anna Kang*
- [ ] **Hug** – *Jez Alborough*
- [ ] **On The Night You Were Born** – *Nancy Tillman*
- [ ] **You Were the First** – *Patricia MacLachlan*
- [ ] **Baby See, Baby Do** – *Robie Rogge*
- [ ] **Baby Dream** – *Sunny Scribens*
- [ ] **Wherever You Are: My Love Will Find You** – *Nancy Tillman*
- [ ] **I Love You, Little Pookie** – *Sandra Boynton*
- [ ] **Tickle, Tickle** – *Helen Oxenbury*
- [ ] **I Love You Through and Through** – *Bernadette Rossetti Shustak*
- [ ] **Fire Truck** – *Peter Sis*

Life, Love, & Family

- [ ] **Do Like Kyla** – *Angela Johnson*
- [ ] **Rain Feet** – *Angela Johnson*
- [ ] **Joshua's Night Whispers** – *Angela Johnson*
- [ ] **Lola at the Library** – *Anna McQuinn*
- [ ] **The Babies and Doggies Book** – *John Schindel & Molly Woodward*
- [ ] **Global Baby Bedtimes** – *Maya Ajmera*
- [ ] **Say Hello!** – *Rachel Isadora*
- [ ] **I Smell Honey** – *Andrea Davis Pinkney*
- [ ] **Leo Can Swim** – *Anna McQuinn*
- [ ] **Leo Loves Baby Time** – *Anna McQuinn*
- [ ] **A Fish to Feed** – *Ellen Mayer*
- [ ] **Red Socks** – *Ellen Mayer*
- [ ] **You and Me, Baby** – *Lynn Reiser*
- [ ] **My Heart Fills With Happiness** – *Monique Gray Smith*
- [ ] **The Going to Bed Book** – *Sandra Boynton*
- [ ] **I Love You to the Moon and Back** – *Amelia Hepworth*
- [ ] **Full, Full, Full of Love** – *Trish Cooke*
- [ ] **We Have a Baby** – *Cathryn Falwell*
- [ ] **Besos for Baby: A Little Book of Kisses** – *Jen Arena*
- [ ] **Baby Says** – *John Steptoe*
- [ ] **Jazz Baby** – *Lisa Wheeler*
- [ ] **Soup Day** – *Melissa Iwai*
- [ ] **Ten, Nine, Eight** – *Molly Bang*
- [ ] **We Are Families** – *Patricia Hegarty*
- [ ] **Carry Me** – *Rena D. Grossman*
- [ ] **"More More More," Said the Baby** – *Vera B Williams*

"You can't keep living without breathing; don't keep living without reading!"

— ERNEST AGYEMANG YEBOAH

- ☐ **Mama, Do You Love Me?** – *Barbara M. Joosse*
- ☐ **Dad By My Side** – *Soosh*
- ☐ **The Family Book** – *Todd Parr*
- ☐ **Food** – *Cathryn Falwell*
- ☐ **Too Pickley!** – *Jean Reidy*
- ☐ **Yummy Yucky** – *Leslie Patricelli*
- ☐ **Eating the Alphabet** – *Lois Ehlert*
- ☐ **Llama Llama Home with Mama** – *Anna Dewdney*
- ☐ **Get Well Soon, Spot** – *Eric Hill*
- ☐ **When Your Elephant Has the Sniffles** – *Susanna Leonard Hill*
- ☐ **How Do You Care for a Very Sick Bear?** – *Vanessa Bayer*

Early Learning

- ☐ **Touchwords: Clothes** – *Rilla Alexander*
- ☐ **10 Little Rubber Ducks** – *Eric Carle*
- ☐ **This Is NOT a Pumpkin** – *Bob Staake*
- ☐ **Mon Petit Busy Day** – *Annette Tamarkin*
- ☐ **Hello Hello** – *Brendan Wenzel*
- ☐ **Little Owl's Night** – *Divya Srinivasan*
- ☐ **Reach** – *"Elizabeth Verdick & Marjorie Lisovskis"*
- ☐ **Orange Pear Apple Bear** – *Emily Gravett*
- ☐ **From Head to Toe** – *Eric Carle*
- ☐ **Say Zoop!** – *Herve Tullet*
- ☐ **Vroom!: It's Color Time!** – *Hunter McKown*
- ☐ **Shapes** – *Jane Cabrera*
- ☐ **City lullaby** – *Marilyn Singer*
- ☐ **Ten Little Fingers and Ten Little Toes** – *Mem Fox*
- ☐ **Bruno Munari's ABC** – *Munari*
- ☐ **Baby's Firsts** – *Nancy Raines Day*
- ☐ **Counting With -Contando Con Frida** – *Patty Rodriguez & Ariana Stein*

- ☐ **Count on the Subway** – *Paul DuBois Jacobs & Jennifer Swender*
- ☐ **Beep Beep** – *Petr Horáček*
- ☐ **Black Bird Yellow Sun** – *Steve Light*
- ☐ **Look, Look!** – *Peter Linenthal*
- ☐ **Charley Harper ABC's** – *Charley Harper*
- ☐ **Flora Forager ABC** – *Bridget Beth Collins*
- ☐ **Before and After** – *Jean Jullien*
- ☐ **Teddy Bedtime** – *Georgie Birkett*
- ☐ **Baby Sees Colors** – *Akio Kashiwara*
- ☐ **Polar Bear, Polar Bear, What Do You Hear?** – *Bill Martin Jr.*
- ☐ **Rumble in the Jungle** – *Giles Andreae*
- ☐ **A B See** – *Elizabeth Doyle*
- ☐ **Toes, Ears, & Nose!** – *Marion Dane Bauer*
- ☐ **Hickory, Dickory, Dock: and other favorite nursery rhymes** – *Tiger Tales*
- ☐ **Quiet Loud** – *Leslie Patricelli*
- ☐ **Freight Train** – *Donald Crews*
- ☐ **Black & White** – *Tana Hoban*

Rhymes, Poems, & Song

- ☐ **Sleeping Bunnies** – *Annie Kubler*
- ☐ **The More We Get Together** – *Caroline Jayne Church*
- ☐ **Charlie Parker Played Be Bop** – *Chris Raschka*
- ☐ **Animal Orchestra** – *Ilo Orleans*
- ☐ **M Is for Music** – *Kathleen Krull*
- ☐ **Goodnight Songs** – *Margaret Wise Brown*
- ☐ **Baby Beluga** – *Raffi*
- ☐ **Down by the Bay** – *Raffi*
- ☐ **Love You Head to Toe** – *Ashley Barron*
- ☐ **The Moon and Me** – *Bear Hands Media*
- ☐ **Haiku Baby** – *Betsy E. Snyder*
- ☐ **Haiku Night** – *Betsy E. Snyder*
- ☐ **I Carry Your Heart with Me** – *E.E. Cummings*
- ☐ **The Owl and the Pussycat** – *Edward Lear*
- ☐ **Thankful** – *Eileen Spinelli*
- ☐ **Tap tap boom boom** – *Elizabeth Bluemle*
- ☐ **Behowl the Moon: An Ageless Story from Shakespeare's A Midsummer Night's Dream** – *Erin Nelsen Parekh & William Shakespeare*
- ☐ **Won't You Be My Neighbor?** – *Fred Rogers*
- ☐ **Snow Still** – *Holly Surplice*
- ☐ **Digger, Dozer, Dumper** – *Hope Vestergaard*

- ☐ **Here Comes Mother Goose** – *Iona Opie*
- ☐ **Read-Aloud Rhymes for the Very Young** – *Jack Prelutsky*
- ☐ **Little Poems for Tiny Ears** – *Lin Oliver*
- ☐ **All the World** – *Liz Garton Scanlon*
- ☐ **I Love All of Me** – *Lorie Ann Grover*
- ☐ **The Runaway Bunny** – *Margaret Wise Brown*
- ☐ **How Do I Love You?** – *Marion Dane Bauer*
- ☐ **Giggly Wiggly: Playtime Rhymes** – *Michael Rosen*
- ☐ **Honey for You, Honey for Me** – *Michael Rosen*
- ☐ **Over in the Meadow** – *Olive A. Wadsworth*
- ☐ **Little You** – *Richard Van Camp*
- ☐ **Summer Evening** – *Walter de la Mare*

Interactive

- ☐ **I Thought I Saw a Bear!** – *Lydia Nichols*
- ☐ **Tails** – *Matthew Van Fleet*
- ☐ **See, Touch, Feel: A First Sensory Book** – *Roger Priddy*
- ☐ **This Book is Magic** – *Ashley Evanson*
- ☐ **Baby Touch Your Nose** – *DK*
- ☐ **Whose Knees are These?** – *Jabari Asim*
- ☐ **TouchThinkLearn: Vehicles** – *Xavier Deneux*
- ☐ **Farm (Touch and Explore)** – *Xavier Deneux*
- ☐ **Open the Barn Door** – *Christopher Santoro*
- ☐ **Where's Spot?** – *Eric Hill*
- ☐ **Baby Touch and Feel (series?)** – *DK*
- ☐ **My First Baby Signs** – *Phil Conigliaro & Tae Won Yu*
- ☐ **Baby Faces** – *Amy Pixton*
- ☐ **Where Is Baby's Belly Button?** – *Karen Katz*
- ☐ **Peek-A Who?** – *Nina Laden*
- ☐ **TouchThinkLearn: ABC** – *Xavier Deneux*
- ☐ **Who?: A Celebration of Babies** – *Robie Harris*
- ☐ **Dig! (Peek-a-Flap Series)** – *Jaye Garnett*

"If you want your children to be intelligent, read them fairy tales. If you want them to be more intelligent, read them more fairy tales."

– ALBERT EINSTEIN

The Natural World

- ☐ **Pond Babies** – *Cathryn Falwell*
- ☐ **All in a Day** – *Cynthia Rylant*
- ☐ **Leaves** – *David Ezra Stein*
- ☐ **Little Tree** – *Jenny Bowers*
- ☐ **Little White Rabbit** – *Kevin Henkes*
- ☐ **Rain!** – *Linda Ashman*
- ☐ **A Good Day for a Hat** – *T. Nat Fuller*
- ☐ **You Are Light** – *Aaron Becker*
- ☐ **Sunrise, Moonrise** – *Betsy Thompson*
- ☐ **Little Owl's Day** – *Divya Srinivasan*
- ☐ **How to Be a Cat** – *Nikki McClure*
- ☐ **Time for Bed** – *Mem Fox*
- ☐ **First Snow** – *Bomi Park*
- ☐ **Little Penguins** – *Cynthia Rylant*
- ☐ **When Spring Comes** – *Kevin Henkes*
- ☐ **Winter is Here** – *Kevin Henkes*
- ☐ **Have You Seen My Duckling?** – *Nancy Tafuri*

Potty Time

- ☐ **Dino Potty** – *Michael Garton*
- ☐ **The Princess and the Potty** – *Wendy Cheyette Lewison*
- ☐ **Let's Go to the Potty!** – *Allison Jandu*
- ☐ **The Potty Book for Girls** – *Alyssa Satin Capucilli*
- ☐ **The Potty Book: For Boys** – *Barbro Lindgren*
- ☐ **Diapers Are Not Forever** – *Elizabeth Verdick*
- ☐ **Big Boy Underpants** – *Fran Manushkin*
- ☐ **Big Girl Panties** – *Fran Manushkin*
- ☐ **Vegetables in Underwear** – *Jared Chapman*
- ☐ **We Poop on the Potty!** – *Jim Harbison & Nicole Sulgit*
- ☐ **My Big Girl Potty** – *Joanna Cole*
- ☐ **A Potty for Me!** – *Karen Katz*
- ☐ **Goldilocks and the Just Right Potty** – *Leigh Hodgkinson*
- ☐ **Daniel Goes to the Potty** – *Maggie Testa*
- ☐ **What Do You Do With A Potty?** – *Marianne Borgardt*
- ☐ **Potty Professional** – *Melissa Sue Walker*
- ☐ **The New Potty** – *Mercer Mayer & Gina Mayer*
- ☐ **P is for Potty!** – *Naomi Kleinberg*
- ☐ **Potty Superhero** – *Parragon Books*
- ☐ **Princess Potty** – *Samantha Berger*
- ☐ **Even Superheroes Use the Potty** – *Sara Crow*

- ☐ **Everyone Poops** – *Taro Gomi*
- ☐ **Even Firefighters Go to the Potty** – *Wendy Wax & Naomi Wax*
- ☐ **Poop! There it is!** – *Xavier Finkley*
- ☐ **Potty** – *Leslie Patricelli*

Silly Stuff

- ☐ **The Full Moon at the Napping House** – *Audrey Wood*
- ☐ **Mustache Baby** – *Bridget Heos*
- ☐ **After the Fall (How Humpty Dumpty Got Back Up Again)** – *Dan Santat*
- ☐ **How do Dinosaurs Say Goodnight?** – *Jane Yolen*
- ☐ **Your Baby's First Word Will Be DADA** – *Jimmy Fallon*
- ☐ **No No Yes Yes** – *Leslie Patricelli*
- ☐ **The Boss Baby** – *Marla Frazee*
- ☐ **Knuffle Bunny** – *Mo Willems*
- ☐ **Welcome** – *Mo Willems*
- ☐ **Hello Ninja** – *N. D. Wilson*
- ☐ **Sheep 101** – *Richard T. Morris*
- ☐ **Blue Hat, Green Hat** – *Sandra Boynton*
- ☐ **But Not the Hippopotamus** – *Sandra Boynton*
- ☐ **Here, George!** – *Sandra Boynton*
- ☐ **Horns to Toes and in Between** – *Sandra Boynton*
- ☐ **Moo Baa La La La** – *Sandra Boynton*
- ☐ **Fly!** – *Mark Teague*

STEAM & Machines

- ☐ **8 Little Planets** – *Chris Ferrie*
- ☐ **Goodnight Lab** – *Chris Ferrie*
- ☐ **Bathtime Mathtime** – *Danica McKellar*
- ☐ **From Seed to Plant** – *Gail Gibbons*
- ☐ **Anatomy for Babies** – *Jonathan Litton*
- ☐ **Apple** – *Nikki McClure*
- ☐ **Baby Loves Quarks!** – *Ruth Spiro*
- ☐ **Baby Code! Art** – *Sandra Horning*
- ☐ **Small Walt** – *Elizabeth Verdick*
- ☐ **Baby Loves Aerospace Engineering!** – *Ruth Spiro*
- ☐ **The Cars and Trucks Book** – *Todd Parr*
- ☐ **Red Truck** – *Kersten Hamilton*
- ☐ **My Truck Is Stuck!** – *Kevin Lewis*
- ☐ **Blue Boat** – *Kersten Hamilton*

AGES 3-6:

Adventure in the Wide World

- ☐ **The Golden Glow** – *Benjamin Flouw*
- ☐ **Three Days on a River in a Red Canoe** – *Vera B Williams*
- ☐ **Ox-Cart Man** – *Donald Hall*
- ☐ **Real Cowboys** – *Kate Hoefler*
- ☐ **A Madeline Treasury** – *Ludwig Bemelmans*
- ☐ **The Adventures of Taxi Dog** – *Debra Barracca & Sal Barracca*
- ☐ **A Pocket for Corduroy** – *Don Freeman*
- ☐ **The Merry Shipwreck** – *Georges Duplaix*
- ☐ **Toot & Puddle** – *Holly Hobbie*
- ☐ **I Am a Bird** – *Hope Lim*
- ☐ **The Maggie B** – *Irene Haas*
- ☐ **Adventures in Brambly Hedge** – *Jill Barklem*
- ☐ **The Wall in the Middle of the Book** – *Jon Agee*
- ☐ **Who Goes There?** – *Karma Wilson*
- ☐ **Sam and Dave Dig a Hole** – *Mac Barnett*
- ☐ **Night of the Moonjellies** – *Mark Shasha*
- ☐ **One-Dog Canoe** – *Mary Casanova*
- ☐ **The Paddington Treasury** – *Michael Bond*
- ☐ **Yellow Kayak** – *Nina Laden*
- ☐ **Flossie and the Fox** – *Patricia McKissack*
- ☐ **One Morning in Maine** – *Robert McCloskey*
- ☐ **Time of Wonder** – *Robert McCloskey*
- ☐ **Max and Ruby's Treasure Hunt** – *Rosemary Wells*
- ☐ **A Lion in Paris** – *Beatrice Alemagna*
- ☐ **ABC: The Alphabet from the Sky** – *Benedikt Gross & Joey Lee*
- ☐ **Metropolis** – *Benoit Tardif*
- ☐ **Come With Me To Paris** – *Gloria Fowler*
- ☐ **The Snail and the Whale** – *Julia Donaldson*
- ☐ **A Walk in London** – *Salvatore Rubbino*
- ☐ **Rain School** – *James Rumford*
- ☐ **This Is How We Do It** – *Matt Lamothe*
- ☐ **Lost and Found** – *Oliver Jeffers*
- ☐ **The Sound of Silence** – *Katrina Goldsaito*

> "If you can imagine something, it will be."
>
> – N. K. JEMISIN

BOOKS WE WANT TO CHECK OUT
Tear out this ticket and take it to the library!

_____

_____

_____

BOOKS WE WANT TO CHECK OUT
Tear out this ticket and take it to the library!

_____

_____

_____

BOOKS WE WANT TO CHECK OUT
Tear out this ticket and take it to the library!

_____

_____

_____

BOOKS WE WANT TO CHECK OUT
Tear out this ticket and take it to the library!

_____

_____

_____

STEAM

- [ ] **Rooster's Off to See the World** – *Eric Carle*
- [ ] **A Kite for Moon** – *Jane Yolen & Heidi E.Y. Stemple*
- [ ] **The Darkest Dark** – *Colonel Chris Hadfield*
- [ ] **Eight Days Gone** – *Linda McReynolds*
- [ ] **Everyone Poops** – *Taro Gomi*
- [ ] **It Looked Like Spilt Milk** – *Charles Shaw*
- [ ] **Mouse Paint** – *Ellen Stoll Walsh*
- [ ] **Little Blue and Little Yellow** – *Leo Lionni*
- [ ] **Extra Yarn** – *Mac Barnett*
- [ ] **What Color Is the Wind?** – *Anne Herbauts*
- [ ] **Everything You Need for a Treehouse** – *Carter Higgins*
- [ ] **Pumpkin Circle: The Story of a Garden** – *George Levenson*
- [ ] **Turtle Pond** – *James Gladstone*
- [ ] **Are You a Dragonfly?** – *Judy Allen*
- [ ] **If You Plant a Seed** – *Kadir Nelson*
- [ ] **Bugs for Lunch** – *Margery Facklam*
- [ ] **Ada Twist, Scientist** – *Andrea Beaty*
- [ ] **Woodpecker Wham!** – *April Pulley Sayre*
- [ ] **The Most Magnificent Thing** – *Ashley Spires*
- [ ] **Maybe Something Beautiful: How Art Transformed a Neighborhood** – *F. Isabel Campoy & Theresa Howell*
- [ ] **Oscar and the Bat: A Book About Sound** – *Geoff Waring*
- [ ] **A Perfectly Messed-Up Story** – *Patrick McDonnell*
- [ ] **Bee Dance** – *Rick Chrustowski*
- [ ] **Hey, Wall: A Story of Art and Community** – *Susan Verde*
- [ ] **Stack the Cats** – *Susie Ghahremani*
- [ ] **I See Myself** – *Vicki Cobb*
- [ ] **Charlotte the Scientist Is Squished** – *Camille Andros*
- [ ] **Beautiful Birds** – *Jean Roussen*
- [ ] **Grandmother Fish** – *Jonathan Tweet*
- [ ] **Insect Detective** – *Steve Voake*
- [ ] **Moon: A Peek-Through Picture Book** – *Britta Teckentrup*
- [ ] **If I Built a House** – *Chris Van Dusen*
- [ ] **Chomp: A Shark Romp** – *Michael Paul*
- [ ] **Wolf Pups Join the Pack** – *American Museum of Natural History*

"Show me a family of readers, and I will show you the people who move the world."

– NAPOLÉON BONAPARTE

- [ ] **Hey, Water!** – *Antoinette Portis*
- [ ] **Bloom Boom!** – *April Pulley Sayre*
- [ ] **National Geographic Little Kids First Big Book of Animals** – *Catherine D. Hughes*
- [ ] **National Geographic Little Kids First Big Book of Dinosaurs** – *Catherine D. Hughes*
- [ ] **National Geographic Little Kids First Big Book of the Ocean** – *Catherine D. Hughes*
- [ ] **Hello, I'm Here!** – *Helen Frost*
- [ ] **Prickly Hedgehogs!** – *Jane McGuinness*
- [ ] **Birds Make Nests** – *Michael Garland*
- [ ] **My Leaf Book** – *Monica Wellington*
- [ ] **Seeds Move!** – *Robin Page*
- [ ] **What Do You Do with a Tail Like This?** – *Steve Jenkins & Robin Page*

Animal Action

- [ ] **The Day Jimmy's Boa Ate the Wash** – *Trinka Hakes Noble*
- [ ] **Town Mouse, Country Mouse** – *Jan Brett*
- [ ] **Our Animal Friends at Maple Hill Farm** – *Alice Provensen & Martin Provensen*
- [ ] **The Salamander Room** – *Anne Mazer*
- [ ] **Squirrels Leap, Squirrels Sleep** – *April Pulley Sayre*
- [ ] **Turtle Splash!: Countdown at the Pond** – *Cathryn Falwell*
- [ ] **Fly High, Fly Low** – *Don Freeman*
- [ ] **My Pet Wants a Pet** – *Elise Broach*
- [ ] **Does a Kangaroo Have a Mother, Too?** – *Eric Carle*
- [ ] **Pete the Cat and His Four Groovy Buttons** – *Eric Litwin*
- [ ] **Pip & Pup** – *Eugene Yelchin*
- [ ] **Dreams** – *Ezra Jack Keats*
- [ ] **Annie and the Wild Animals** – *Jan Brett*
- [ ] **Hedgie's Surprise** – *Jan Brett*

- ☐ **Jan Brett's Animal Treasury** – *Jan Brett*
- ☐ **Bear Snores On** – *Karma Wilson*
- ☐ **Bear Wants More** – *Karma Wilson*
- ☐ **A Perfect Day** – *Lane Smith*
- ☐ **It's Mine!** – *Leo Lionni*
- ☐ **The Lion and the Bird** – *Marianne Dubuc*
- ☐ **Hattie and the Fox** – *Mem Fox*
- ☐ **Hello Baby!** – *Mem Fox*
- ☐ **The Best Nest** – *P.D. Eastman*
- ☐ **The Brownstone** – *Paula Scher*
- ☐ **Richard Scarry's Busytown Treasury** – *Richard Scarry*
- ☐ **Please, Mr. Panda** – *Steve Antony*
- ☐ **The Color Box** – *Dayle Ann Dodds*
- ☐ **The Stray Dog** – *Marc Simont*
- ☐ **Duck on a Bike** – *David Shannon*
- ☐ **Duck in the Truck** – *Jez Alborough*
- ☐ **The Very Busy Spider** – *Eric Carle*
- ☐ **Bark, George** – *Jules Feiffer*
- ☐ **Stellaluna** – *Janell Cannon*
- ☐ **Ask Mr. Bear** – *Marjorie Flack*
- ☐ **Mama Cat Has Three Kittens** – *Denise Fleming*
- ☐ **Angelina Ballerina** – *Katharine Holabird*
- ☐ **Widget** – *Lyn Rossiter McFarland*
- ☐ **Doctor De Soto** – *William Steig*
- ☐ **Biscuit Loves the Library** – *Alyssa Satin Capucilli*
- ☐ **Library Lion** – *Michelle Knudsen*
- ☐ **How Rocket Learned to Read** – *Tad Hills*
- ☐ **Geraldine** – *Elizabeth Lilly*
- ☐ **Leo the Late Bloomer** – *Robert Munsch*
- ☐ **Owl Babies** – *Martin Waddell*

Timeless Classics

- ☐ **Curious George** – *H.A. Rey*
- ☐ **We're Going on a Bear Hunt** – *Helen Oxenbury*
- ☐ **Alligators All Around** – *Maurice Sendak*
- ☐ **Go Away, Big Green Monster!** – *Ed Emberley*
- ☐ **Each Peach Pear Plum** – *Allan Ahlberg*
- ☐ **Don't Let the Pigeon Drive the Bus!** – *Mo Willems*
- ☐ **Cloudy With a Chance of Meatballs** – *Judi Barrett*
- ☐ **Blueberries for Sal** – *Robert McCloskey*
- ☐ **Miss Rumphius** – *Barbara Cooney*
- ☐ **The Classic Tale of Peter Rabbit** – *Beatrix Potter*
- ☐ **Lyle, Lyle, Crocodile** – *Bernard Waber*

"Make reading your hobby, even if you don't like to read. You will learn things that will prove useful when you least expect it!"

– NEELABH PRATAP SINGH

- ☐ **Strega Nona** – *Tomie de Paola*
- ☐ **Madeline** – *Ludwig Bemelmans*
- ☐ **A Bear Called Paddington** – *Michael Bond*
- ☐ **Harold and the Purple Crayon** – *Crockett Johnson*
- ☐ **Make Way for Ducklings** – *Robert McCloskey*
- ☐ **The Story of Babar** – *Jean De Brunhoff*
- ☐ **The Paper Bag Princess** – *Robert Munsch*
- ☐ **The Tale of Peter Rabbit** – *Beatrix Potter*
- ☐ **Horton Hatches the Egg** – *Dr. Seuss*
- ☐ **Harry the Dirty Dog** – *Gene Zion*
- ☐ **The Mitten** – *Jan Brett*
- ☐ **Bread and Jam for Frances** – *Russell Hoban*
- ☐ **The Velveteen Rabbit** – *Margery Williams*
- ☐ **Caps for Sale** – *Esphyr Slobodkina*
- ☐ **Frog and Toad Are Friends** – *Arnold Lobel*
- ☐ **The Little Mouse, the Red Ripe Strawberry, and the Big Hungry Bear** – *Don Wood*
- ☐ **The Ugly Duckling** – *Hans Christian Andersen*
- ☐ **Where the Wild Things Are** – *Maurice Sendak*
- ☐ **The Doorbell Rang** – *Pat Hutchins*
- ☐ **The Giving Tree** – *Shel Silverstein*
- ☐ **The Little House** – *Virginia Lee Burton*
- ☐ **Henny Penny** – *Paul Galdone*
- ☐ **Jack and the Beanstalk** – *Paul Galdone*
- ☐ **Little Red Riding Hood** – *Paul Galdone*
- ☐ **The Little Red Hen** – *Paul Galdone*
- ☐ **Green Eggs and Ham** – *Dr. Seuss*
- ☐ **Owl Moon** – *Jane Yolen*
- ☐ **Amelia Bedelia** – *Peggy Parish*
- ☐ **If You Give a Moose a Muffin** – *Laura Numeroff*
- ☐ **The Cat in the Hat** – *Dr. Seuss*
- ☐ **The Story of Ferdinand** – *Munro Leaf*
- ☐ **The Kissing Hand** – *Audrey Penn*

BOOKS WE WANT TO CHECK OUT
Tear out this ticket and take it to the library!

_____

_____

_____

BOOKS WE WANT TO CHECK OUT
Tear out this ticket and take it to the library!

_____

_____

_____

BOOKS WE WANT TO CHECK OUT
Tear out this ticket and take it to the library!

_____

_____

_____

BOOKS WE WANT TO CHECK OUT
Tear out this ticket and take it to the library!

_____

_____

_____

- [ ] **Are You My Mother?** – *P.D. Eastman*
- [ ] **The Three Little Pigs** – *Paul Galdone*
- [ ] **Alexander and the Terrible** – *Judith Viorst*
- [ ] **If You Give a Mouse a Cookie** – *Laura Numeroff*
- [ ] **Corduroy** – *Don Freeman*

Silly Stuff

- [ ] **The Bad Seed** – *Jory John*
- [ ] **Splat the Cat: I Scream for Ice Cream** – *Rob Scotton*
- [ ] **Pigs Aplenty, Pigs Galore** – *David McPhail*
- [ ] **Good Night iPad** – *Ann Droyd*
- [ ] **No, David!** – *David Shannon*
- [ ] **The Snatchabook** – *Helen Docherty*
- [ ] **The Wonky Donkey** – *Craig Smith*
- [ ] **Pumpkin Trouble** – *Jan Thomas*
- [ ] **Naughty Little Monkeys** – *Jim Aylesworth*
- [ ] **This Is Not My Hat** – *Jon Klassen*
- [ ] **We Found a Hat** – *Jon Klassen*
- [ ] **Z Is for Moose** – *Kelly Bingham*
- [ ] **The Seven Silly Eaters** – *Mary Ann Hoberman*
- [ ] **Pirates Don't Change Diapers** – *Melinda Long*
- [ ] **Edwina, the Dinosaur Who Didn't Know She Was Extinct** – *Mo Willems*
- [ ] **There Is a Bird On Your Head!** – *Mo Willems*
- [ ] **We Are in a Book!** – *Mo Willems*
- [ ] **Officer Buckle & Gloria** – *Peggy Rathmann*
- [ ] **We Don't Eat Our Classmates** – *Ryan T. Higgins*
- [ ] **Mrs. McNosh Hangs Up Her Wash** – *Sarah Weeks*
- [ ] **Wordy Birdy** – *Tammi Sauer*
- [ ] **Shifty McGifty and Slippery Sam** – *Tracey Corderoy*
- [ ] **Froggy Gets Dressed** – *Jonathan London*
- [ ] **Animals Should Definitely Not Wear Clothing** – *Judi Barrett*

- [ ] **Rhyming Dust Bunnies** – *Jan Thomas*
- [ ] **Hi, Pizza Man!** – *Virginia Walter*
- [ ] **There Was an Old Lady Who Swallowed a Fly** – *Lucille Colandro*
- [ ] **The Lady with the Alligator Purse** – *Mary Ann Hoberman*
- [ ] **Whose Mouse are You?** – *Robert Kraus*
- [ ] **The Important Book** – *Margaret Wise Brown*
- [ ] **Trashy Town** – *Andrea Zimmerman & David Clemesha*
- [ ] **If I Never Forever Endeavor** – *Holly Meade*
- [ ] **The Neighborhood Mother Goose** – *Nina Crews*
- [ ] **Baby-Boo, I Love You** – *Sheryl Haft*
- [ ] **¡Pío Peep!: Traditional Spanish Nursery Rhymes** – *Alma Flor Ada & F. Isabel Campoy & Alice Schertle*
- [ ] **A Poem for Peter** – *Andrea Davis Pinkney*
- [ ] **DOGKU** – *Andrew Clements*
- [ ] **The Scarecrow** – *Beth Ferry*
- [ ] **A Stone Sat Still** – *Brendan Wenzel*
- [ ] **Shout!: Little Poems that Roar** – *Brod Bagert*
- [ ] **Over in the Wetlands: A Hurricane-on-the-Bayou Story** – *Caroline Starr Rose*
- [ ] **H.O.R.S.E.** – *Christopher Myers*
- [ ] **Things to Do** – *Elaine Magliaro*
- [ ] **A Greyhound, a Groundhog** – *Emily Jenkins*
- [ ] **TWILIGHT CHANT** – *Holly Thompson*
- [ ] **The 20th Century Children's Poetry Treasury** – *Jack Prelutsky*
- [ ] **Here's A Little Poem** – *Jane Yolen & Andrew Fusek Peters*
- [ ] **Rhyme Crime** – *Jon Burgerman*
- [ ] **Before Morning** – *Joyce Sidman*
- [ ] **A HOUSE THAT ONCE WAS** – *Julie Fogliano*
- [ ] **A Dance Like Starlight** – *Kristy Dempsey*
- [ ] **My People** – *Langston Hughes*
- [ ] **That Is My Dream!** – *Langston Hughes*
- [ ] **Lion of the Sky: Haiku for All Seasons** – *Laura Purdie Salas*
- [ ] **Snowman - Cold = Puddle: Spring Equations** – *Laura Purdie Salas*
- [ ] **Won Ton: A Cat Tale Told in Haiku** – *Lee Wardlaw*
- [ ] **Feelings & Friendship** – *Libby Walden*
- [ ] **Waiting for Wings** – *Lois Ehlert*

"There is no such thing as a child who hates to read; there are only children who have not found the right book."

— FRANK SERAFINI

- ☐ **Chicken Soup with Rice** – *Maurice Sendak*
- ☐ **I See the Moon** – *Nosy Crow*
- ☐ **Firefly July** – *Paul B. Janeczko*
- ☐ **A Child's Garden of Verses** – *Robert Louis Stevenson*
- ☐ **The Land of Nod** – *Robert Louis Stevenson*
- ☐ **Poetree** – *Shauna LaVoy Reynolds*
- ☐ **The House in the Night** – *Susan Marie Swanson*
- ☐ **A Hatful of Dragons** – *Vikram Madan*
- ☐ **One Duck Stuck** – *Phyllis Root*
- ☐ **Truckery Rhymes** – *Jon Scieszka*
- ☐ **Sheep in a Jeep** – *Nancy E. Shaw*
- ☐ **Rain Makes Applesauce** – *Julian Scheer*
- ☐ **Is Your Mama a Llama?** – *Deborah Guarino*
- ☐ **Tomorrow Most Likely** – *Dave Eggers*
- ☐ **Daniel Finds a Poem** – *Micha Archer*

Be Yourself

- ☐ **Philea's Fortune: A Story About Self-Expression** – *Agnes De Lestrade*
- ☐ **What I Like About Me!** – *Allia Zobel Nolan*
- ☐ **Dear Girl,** – *Amy Krouse Rosenthal & Paris Rosenthal*
- ☐ **The Magical Yet** – *Angela DiTerlizzi*
- ☐ **What Can I Be?** – *Ann Rand*
- ☐ **Quick As a Cricket** – *Audrey Wood*
- ☐ **You Matter** – *Christian Robinson*
- ☐ **Willow** – *Denise Brennan-Nelson & Rosemarie Brennan*
- ☐ **Crown: An Ode to the Fresh Cut** – *Derrick Barnes*
- ☐ **I Am Every Good Thing** – *Derrick Barnes*
- ☐ **Rufus the Writer** – *Elizabeth Bram*
- ☐ **Ladybug Girl** – *Jacky Davis*
- ☐ **Alma and How She Got Her Name** – *Juana Martinez-Neal*
- ☐ **I Like Myself!** – *Karen Beaumont*

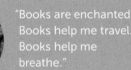

"Books are enchanted. Books help me travel. Books help me breathe."

— MARGARITA ENGLE

- ☐ **Duddle Puck: The Puddle Duck** – *Karma Wilson*
- ☐ **Hilda Must Be Dancing** – *Karma Wilson*
- ☐ **Green Pants** – *Kenneth Kraegel*
- ☐ **Lola Dutch** – *Kenneth Wright*
- ☐ **Chrysanthemum** – *Kevin Henkes*
- ☐ **Sheila Rae, the Brave** – *Kevin Henkes*
- ☐ **An Extraordinary Egg** – *Leo Lionni*
- ☐ **Xander's Panda Party** – *Linda Sue Park*
- ☐ **Spaghetti in a Hot Dog Bun: Having the Courage To Be Who You Are** – *Maria Dismondy*
- ☐ **Be Brave Little One** – *Marianne Richmond*
- ☐ **Leonardo, the Terrible Monster** – *Mo Willems*
- ☐ **Roberto: The Insect Architect** – *Nina Laden*
- ☐ **Stand Tall, Molly Lou Melon** – *Patty Lovell*
- ☐ **The Invisible Boy** – *Trudy Ludwig*
- ☐ **Just Like Me** – *Vanessa Brantley-Newton*

Who We Are

- ☐ **Ambitious Girl** – *Meena Harris*
- ☐ **Little Red** – *Bethan Woollvin*
- ☐ **Hands Up!** – *Breanna J. McDaniel*
- ☐ **Not All Princesses Dress in Pink** – *Jane Yolen & Heidi E. Y. Stemple*
- ☐ **Grace for President** – *Kelly DiPucchio*
- ☐ **Drum Dream Girl** – *Margarita Engle*
- ☐ **Sofia Valdez, Future Prez** – *Andrea Beaty*
- ☐ **Marisol McDonald Doesn't Match** – *Monica Brown*
- ☐ **The Ugly Vegetables** – *Grace Lin*
- ☐ **Flower Garden** – *Eve Bunting*
- ☐ **Mommy's Khimar** – *Jamilah Thompkins-Bigelow*
- ☐ **The Skin You Live In** – *Michael Tyler*
- ☐ **Ninja!** – *Arree Chung*
- ☐ **Abuela** – *Arthur Dorros*
- ☐ **Lovely** – *Jess Hong*
- ☐ **Julián is a Mermaid** – *Jessica Love*
- ☐ **Hello, America!** – *Martha Zschock*
- ☐ **My Daddy, Dr. Martin Luther King, Jr.** – *Martin Luther King III*
- ☐ **Goin' Someplace Special** – *Patricia C. McKissack*
- ☐ **Say Hello!** – *Rachel Isadora*
- ☐ **We Are Grateful: Otsaliheliga** – *Traci Sorell*
- ☐ **Danbi Leads the School Parade** – *Anna Kim*
- ☐ **Freedom in Congo Square** – *Carole Boston Weatherford*

- ☐ **Dumpling Dreams: How Joyce Chen Brought the Dumpling from Beijing to Cambridge** – *Carrie Clickard*
- ☐ **Suki's Kimono** – *Chieri Uegaki*
- ☐ **The Little Red Lighthouse and the Great Gray Bridge** – *Hildegarde H. Swift*
- ☐ **Your Name Is a Song** – *Jamilah Thompkins-Bigelow*
- ☐ **All Because You Matter** – *Tami Charles*
- ☐ **The Name Jar** – *Yangsook Choi*

"Let us remember: one book, one pen, one child, and one teacher can change the world."

– MALALA YOUSAFZEI

Contemporary Classics

- ☐ **Click, Clack, Moo Cows That Type** – *Doreen Cronin*
- ☐ **The Day the Crayons Quit** – *Drew Daywalt*
- ☐ **Press Here** – *Herve Tullet*
- ☐ **The Tortoise and the Hare** – *Jerry Pinkney*
- ☐ **The Tiger Who Came to Tea** – *Judith Kerr*
- ☐ **Lilly's Purple Plastic Purse** – *Kevin Henkes*
- ☐ **Last Stop on Market Street** – *Matt de la Peña*
- ☐ **Thank You, Omu!** – *Oge Mora*
- ☐ **Here We Are: Notes for Living on Planet Earth** – *Oliver Jeffers*
- ☐ **Dragons Love Tacos** – *Adam Rubin*
- ☐ **The Book with No Pictures** – *B. J. Novak*
- ☐ **They All Saw A Cat** – *Brendan Wenzel*
- ☐ **The Day You Begin** – *Jacqueline Woodson*
- ☐ **Skippyjon Jones** – *Judy Schachner*
- ☐ **Mr. Tiger Goes Wild** – *Peter Brown*
- ☐ **The Dot** – *Peter H Reynolds*
- ☐ **Pinkalicious** – *Victoria Kann & Elizabeth Kann*
- ☐ **I Want My Hat Back** – *Jon Klassen*
- ☐ **The Gruffalo** – *Julia Donaldson*
- ☐ **Pete the Cat: I Love My White Shoes** – *Eric Litwin*
- ☐ **Fancy Nancy** – *Jane O'Connor*
- ☐ **The Hat** – *Jan Brett*

Wordless

- ☐ **The Lion and the Mouse** – *Jerry Pinkney*
- ☐ **Imagine!** – *Raúl Colón*
- ☐ **Tuesday** – *David Wiesner*
- ☐ **The Snowman** – *Raymond Briggs*
- ☐ **Anno's Journey** – *Mitsumasa Anno*
- ☐ **Journey** – *Aaron Becker*
- ☐ **Museum Trip** – *Barbara Lehman*

- ☐ **Rainstorm** – *Barbara Lehman*
- ☐ **The Red Book** – *Barbara Lehman*
- ☐ **Chalk** – *Bill Thomson*
- ☐ **Fossil** – *Bill Thomson*
- ☐ **The Typewriter** – *Bill Thomson*
- ☐ **A Ball for Daisy** – *Chris Raschka*
- ☐ **Float** – *Daniel Miyares*
- ☐ **Night Out** – *Daniel Miyares*
- ☐ **That Neighbor Kid** – *Daniel Miyares*
- ☐ **Flotsam** – *Raymond Briggs*
- ☐ **Stormy: A Story About Finding a Forever Home** – *Guojing*
- ☐ **One Little Bag: An Amazing Journey** – *Henry Cole*
- ☐ **Spot, the Cat** – *Henry Cole*
- ☐ **Unspoken: A Story From the Underground Railroad** – *Henry Cole*
- ☐ **Found** – *Jeff Newman*
- ☐ **The Fisherman & the Whale** – *Jessica Lanan*
- ☐ **I Walk with Vanessa** – *Kerascoët*
- ☐ **Flashlight** – *Lizi Boyd*
- ☐ **A Boy, a Dog, and a Frog** – *Mercer Maye*
- ☐ **Flora and the Flamingo** – *Molly Idle*
- ☐ **Hike** – *Pete Oswald*
- ☐ **Rain** – *Peter Spier*
- ☐ **The Adventures of Polo** – *Regis Faller*
- ☐ **Wallpaper** – *Thao Lam*
- ☐ **Pancakes for Breakfast** – *Tomie dePaola*

Trains, Planes, & Big Machines

- ☐ **The Little Engine That Could** – *Watty Piper*
- ☐ **Subway** – *Christoph Niemann*
- ☐ **Skyscraper** – *Jorey Hurley*
- ☐ **Dreaming Up: A Celebration of Building** – *Christy Hale*
- ☐ **Ty's Travels: All Aboard!** – *Kelly Starling Lyons*

- [ ] **Scuffy the Tugboat** – *Gertrude Crampton*
- [ ] **If I Built a Car** – *Chris Van Dusen*
- [ ] **Alphabet Trucks** – *Samantha R. Vamos*
- [ ] **Underground: Subway Systems Around the World** – *Uijung Kim*
- [ ] **Mike Mulligan and His Steam Shovel** – *Virginia Lee Burton*
- [ ] **I Stink!** – *Kate McMullan*
- [ ] **Cars and Trucks and Things That Go** – *Richard Scarry*
- [ ] **Steam Train, Dream Train** – *Sherri Duskey Rinker*
- [ ] **Blue Boat** – *Kersten Hamilton*

Life, Love, & Family

- [ ] **Jesse Bear, What Will You Wear?** – *Nancy White Carlstrom*
- [ ] **City Shapes** – *Diana Murray*
- [ ] **In Plain Sight** – *Richard Jackson*
- [ ] **Lottie Paris and the Best Place** – *Angela Johnson*
- [ ] **All the Way to Havana** – *Margarita Engle*
- [ ] **Saturday** – *Oge Mora*
- [ ] **Magic Beach** – *Alison Lester*
- [ ] **Island Boy** – *Barbara Cooney*
- [ ] **Three Pebbles and A Song** – *Eileen Spinelli*
- [ ] **Mister Seahorse** – *Eric Carle*
- [ ] **Peter's Chair** – *Ezra Jack Keats*
- [ ] **Julius, the Baby of the World** – *Kevin Henkes*
- [ ] **Bee-Bim Bop!** – *Linda Sue Park*
- [ ] **Growing Vegetable Soup** – *Lois Ehlert*
- [ ] **Koala Lou** – *Mem Fox*
- [ ] **Just Me and My Dad** – *Mercer Mayer*
- [ ] **Fred Stays With Me!** – *Nancy Coffelt*
- [ ] **The Bee Tree** – *Patricia Polacco*
- [ ] **Thunder Cake** – *Patricia Polacco*
- [ ] **Elizabeti's Doll** – *Stephanie Stuve-Bodeen*
- [ ] **Grandma's Purse** – *Vanessa Brantley-Newton*
- [ ] **A Chair for My Mother** – *Vera B Williams*
- [ ] **Can't You Sleep, Little Bear?** – *Martin Waddell*
- [ ] **The Favorite Daughter** – *Allen Say*
- [ ] **Bigmama's** – *Donald Crews*
- [ ] **Flora's Very Windy Day** – *Jeanne Birdsall*
- [ ] **Finding Grandma's Memories** – *Jiyeon Pak*
- [ ] **Our Favorite Day** – *Joowon Oh*
- [ ] **Storm in the Night** – *Mary Stolz*
- [ ] **Tia Isa Wants a Car** – *Meg Medina*

"The whole world opened up to me when I learned to read."

– MARY MCCLEOD BETHUNE

- [ ] **Night Noises** – *Mem Fox*
- [ ] **While Grandpa Naps** – *Naomi Danis*
- [ ] **When Father Comes Home** – *Sarah Jung*
- [ ] **Mei-Mei's Lucky Birthday Noodles: A Loving Story of Adoption, Chinese Culture and a Special Birthday Treat** – *Shan-Shan Chen*
- [ ] **The Berenstain Bears and the Messy Room** – *Stan Berenstain & Jan Berenstain*
- [ ] **The Invisible String** – *Patrice Karst*
- [ ] **The Relatives Came** – *Cynthia Rylant*
- [ ] **Families, Families, Families** – *Suzanne Lang*
- [ ] **Buzz** – *Janet S. Wong*
- [ ] **Noisy Nora** – *Rosemary Wells*
- [ ] **Thunder Boy Jr.** – *Sherman Alexie*
- [ ] **Wolfie the Bunny** – *Ame Dyckman*
- [ ] **The New Small Person** – *Lauren Child*
- [ ] **I Got the School Spirit** – *Connie Schofield-Morrison*
- [ ] **One Green Apple** – *Eve Bunting*
- [ ] **Skippyjon Jones, Class Action** – *Judy Schachner*
- [ ] **The Smallest Girl in the Smallest Grade** – *Justin Roberts*
- [ ] **Germs Make Me Sick!** – *Melvin Berger*
- [ ] **Dragons Get Colds Too** – *Rebecca Roan*
- [ ] **Don't You Feel Well, Sam?** – *Amy Hest*
- [ ] **Bob Not Bob!** – *Audrey Vernick & Liz Garton Scanlon*
- [ ] **The Sniffles for Bear** – *Bonny Becker*
- [ ] **Monkey and Elephant Get Better** – *Carole Lexa Schaefer*
- [ ] **When You're Feeling Sick** – *Coy Bowles*
- [ ] **A Bad Case of Stripes** – *David Shannon*
- [ ] **Felicity Floo Visits the Zoo** – *E.S. Redmond*
- [ ] **My Mommy Medicine** – *Edwidge Danticat*
- [ ] **How Do Dinosaurs Get Well Soon?** – *Jane Yolen*

- ☐ **Bear Feels Sick** – *Karma Wilson*
- ☐ **Mogie: The Heart of the House** – *Kathi Appelt*
- ☐ **I Want to Be A Doctor** – *Laura Driscoll*
- ☐ **Dear Daisy, Get Well Soon** – *Maggie Smith*
- ☐ **A Sick Day for Amos McGee** – *Philip C. Stead*

Stories Handed Down

- ☐ **The Orphan: A Cinderella Story from Greece** – *Anthony Manna & Christodoula Mitakidou*
- ☐ **Brothers of the Knight** – *Debbie Allen*
- ☐ **Lon Po Po: A Red-Riding Hood Story from China** – *Ed Young*
- ☐ **The Country Mouse and the City Mouse** – *Eric Blair*
- ☐ **Raven: A Trickster Tale from the Pacific Northwest** – *Gerald McDermott*
- ☐ **Tiny Feet Between the Mountains** – *Hanna Cha*
- ☐ **Goldilocks and the Three Bears** – *James Marshall*
- ☐ **Juan Bobo Goes to Work** – *Marisa Montes*
- ☐ **Very Short Fables to Read Together** – *Mary Ann Hoberman*
- ☐ **Puss in Boots** – *Paul Galdone*
- ☐ **The Ant & The Grasshopper** – *R.F. Gilmor*
- ☐ **The Tortoise and the Hare** – *Teresa Mlawer*
- ☐ **Anansi and the Moss-Covered Rock** – *Eric A. Kimmel*
- ☐ **The Turnip** – *Jan Brett*
- ☐ **Seven Blind Mice** – *Ed Young*
- ☐ **The Three Pigs** – *David Wiesner*
- ☐ **The Talking Eggs** – *Robert D. San Souci*
- ☐ **Farmer Duck** – *Martin Waddell*
- ☐ **Anansi the Spider: A Tale from the Ashanti** – *Eric A. Kimmel*
- ☐ **The Tale Of Tricky Fox** – *Jim Aylesworth*
- ☐ **The True Story of the 3 Little Pigs** – *Jon Scieszka*
- ☐ **The Folk Tale Classics Treasury** – *Paul Galdone*

> "I have always imagined that paradise will be a kind of library."
>
> – JORGE LUIS BORGES

- ☐ **Bringing the Rain to Kapiti Plain** – *Verna Aardema*
- ☐ **The Wolf's Chicken Stew** – *Keiko Kasza*

Magic & Fairy Tales

- ☐ **The Stinky Cheese Man and Other Fairly Stupid Tales** – *Jon Scieszka*
- ☐ **James Marshall's Cinderella** – *Barbara Karlin*
- ☐ **Sleeping Beauty** – *Carol Ottolenghi*
- ☐ **The Adventures of Beekle: The Unimaginary Friend** – *Dan Santat*
- ☐ **The Gingerbread Man** – *Eric A. Kimmel*
- ☐ **The Elves and the Shoemaker** – *Paul Galdone*
- ☐ **Little Red and the Very Hungry Lion** – *Alex T. Smith*
- ☐ **Maya and the Turtle: A Korean Fairy Tales** – *John C. Stickler & Soma Han*
- ☐ **Roxaboxen** – *Alice McLerran*
- ☐ **Interstellar Cinderella** – *Deborah Underwood*
- ☐ **Reading Beauty** – *Deborah Underwood*
- ☐ **The Ghanaian Goldilocks** – *Dr Tamara Pizzoli*
- ☐ **The Paper Kingdom** – *Helena Ku Rhee*
- ☐ **Cinders: A Chicken Cinderella** – *Jan Brett*
- ☐ **Little Red Writing** – *Joan Holub*
- ☐ **It's Not Hansel and Gretel** – *Josh Funk*
- ☐ **Room on the Broom** – *Julia Donaldson*
- ☐ **The Wish Tree** – *Kyo Maclear*
- ☐ **Falling for Rapunzel** – *Leah Wilcox*
- ☐ **Goldilocks and Just the One Bear** – *Leigh Hodgkinson*
- ☐ **Goldilocks and the Three Dinosaurs** – *Mo Willems*
- ☐ **Goldy Luck and the Three Pandas** – *Natasha Yim*
- ☐ **The Three Billy Goats Gruff** – *Paul Galdone*
- ☐ **Puff, the Magic Dragon** – *Peter Yarrow & Lenny Lipton*
- ☐ **Rapunzel** – *Rachel Isadora*
- ☐ **Beauty & the Beast** – *Robert Sabuda*
- ☐ **La Princesa and the Pea** – *Susan Middleton Elya*
- ☐ **Little Red Gliding Hood** – *Tara Lazar*
- ☐ **Ocean Meets Sky** – *Terry Fan & Eric Fan*
- ☐ **The Night Gardener** – *Terry Fan & Eric Fan*
- ☐ **Adelita** – *Tomie dePaola*
- ☐ **The Knight and the Dragon** – *Tomie dePaola*

Social Emotional

- [ ] **A Mother for Choco** – *Keiko Kasza*
- [ ] **The Hello, Goodbye Window** – *Norton Juster*
- [ ] **Amazing Grace** – *Mary Hoffman*
- [ ] **My Friend Rabbit** – *Eric Rohmann*
- [ ] **I Wish You More** – *Amy Krouse Rosenthal*
- [ ] **Land Shark** – *Beth Ferry*
- [ ] **Ida, Always** – *Caron Levis*
- [ ] **Shy Willow** – *Cat Min*
- [ ] **Me & Mama** – *Cozbi A. Cabrera*
- [ ] **Saturday Is Swimming Day** – *Hyewon Yum*
- [ ] **You Are a Lion!: And Other Fun Yoga Poses** – *Taeeun Yoo*
- [ ] **That's Me Loving You** – *Amy Krouse Rosenthal*
- [ ] **I Love You the Purplest** – *Barbara Joosse*
- [ ] **Have You Filled a Bucket Today?** – *Carol McCloud*
- [ ] **Jabari Jumps** – *Gaia Cornwall*
- [ ] **Maybe I Can Love My Neighbor Too** – *Jennifer Grant*
- [ ] **Ruby In Her Own Time** – *Jonathan Emmett*
- [ ] **Penguin Problems** – *Jory John*
- [ ] **Let Me Hold You Longer** – *Karen Kingsbury*
- [ ] **La La La: A Story of Hope** – *Kate DiCamillo*
- [ ] **A Good Day** – *Kevin Henkes*
- [ ] **Owen** – *Kevin Henkes*
- [ ] **What Do You Do With an Idea?** – *Kobi Yamada*
- [ ] **Before You Were Mine** – *Maribeth Boelts*
- [ ] **Scaredy Squirrel at Night** – *Mélanie Watt*
- [ ] **Skin You Live In** – *Michael Tyler*
- [ ] **Hair Love** – *Matthew A. Cherry*
- [ ] **I Love You, Stinky Face** – *Lisa Mccourt*
- [ ] **Tomorrow I'll Be Brave** – *Jessica Hische*
- [ ] **Lots of Feelings & Friendship** – *Shelley Rotner*

Feelings & Friendship

- [ ] **If I Had a Little Dream** – *Nina Laden*
- [ ] **Sophie's Squash** – *Pat Zietlow Miller*

> "Reading is a discount ticket to everywhere."
>
> – MARY SCHMICH

- [ ] **The Color Monster** – *Anna Llenas*
- [ ] **Elmore** – *Holly Hobbie*
- [ ] **Owen & Mzee: The True Story of a Remarkable Friendship** – *Isabella Hatkoff & Craig Hatkoff & Paula Kahumbu*
- [ ] **The Berenstain Bears: Kindness Counts** – *Jan Berenstain & Mike Berenstain*
- [ ] **Duck Says Don't** – *Alison Richie*
- [ ] **Me, Toma and the Concrete Garden** – *Andrew Larsen*
- [ ] **Boxes for Katje** – *Candace Fleming*
- [ ] **The Little Yellow Leaf** – *Carin Berger*
- [ ] **Hattie and Hudson** – *Chris Van Dusen*
- [ ] **The Rabbit Listened** – *Cori Doerrfeld*
- [ ] **The Monster Princess** – *D.J. MacHale*
- [ ] **Rabbit & Possum** – *Dana Wulfekotte*
- [ ] **In a Jar** – *Deborah Marcero*
- [ ] **Enemy Pie** – *Derek Munson*
- [ ] **Words Are Not for Hurting** – *Elizabeth Verdick*
- [ ] **Apt. 3** – *Ezra Jack Keats*
- [ ] **Whistle for Willie** – *Ezra Jack Keats*
- [ ] **That's My Carrot** – *Il Sung Na*
- [ ] **A House in the Woods** – *Inga Moore*
- [ ] **Juna's Jar** – *Jane Bahk*
- [ ] **My Friend Bear** – *Jez Alborough*
- [ ] **Fish is Fish** – *Leo Lionni*
- [ ] **Swimmy** – *Leo Lionni*
- [ ] **Maisy Goes to Preschool** – *Lucy Cousins*
- [ ] **Roller Coaster** – *Marla Frazee*
- [ ] **Bear Has a Story to Tell** – *Philip C. Stead*
- [ ] **Samson in the Snow** – *Philip C. Stead*
- [ ] **Hug Me** – *Simona Ciraolo*
- [ ] **Pie Is for Sharing** – *Stephanie Parsley Ledyard*
- [ ] **What Are You So Grumpy About?** – *Tom Lichtenheld*
- [ ] **Rufus: The Bat Who Loved Colors** – *Tomi Ungerer*
- [ ] **The Caterpillar and the Polliwog** – *Jack Kent*
- [ ] **A Visitor for Bear** – *Bonny Becker*
- [ ] **Happy Birthday, Moon** – *Frank Asch*
- [ ] **Animal Action** – *Ian Falconer*
- [ ] **Where's My Teddy?** – *Jez Alborough*
- [ ] **The Word Collector** – *Peter H. Reynolds*
- [ ] **Bunny Cakes** – *Rosemary Wells*
- [ ] **The Storm Whale** – *Benji Davies*
- [ ] **Joseph Had a Little Overcoat** – *Simms Taback*

"A book, too, can be a star, a living fire to lighten the darkness, leading out into the expanding universe."

— MADELEINE L'ENGLE

Nature & the Natural World

- [ ] **Lola Plants a Garden** – *Anna McQuinn*
- [ ] **A Color of His Own** – *Leo Lionni*
- [ ] **Otis** – *Loren Long*
- [ ] **One Day in the Eucalyptus, Eucalyptus Tree** – *Daniel Bernstrom*
- [ ] **Florette** – *Anna Walker*
- [ ] **First the Egg** – *Laura Vaccaro Seeger*
- [ ] **Outside Your Window: A First Book of Nature & the Natural World** – *Nicola Davies*
- [ ] **In the Rain with Baby Duck** – *Amy Hest*
- [ ] **Farewell to Shady Glade** – *Bill Peet*
- [ ] **The Red Lemon** – *Bob Staake*
- [ ] **Night in the Country** – *Cynthia Rylant*
- [ ] **In the Small, Small Pond** – *Denise Fleming*
- [ ] **A Nest Is Noisy** – *Dianna Hutts Aston*
- [ ] **An Egg Is Quiet** – *Dianna Hutts Aston*
- [ ] **Blue on Blue** – *Dianne White*
- [ ] **Miss Maple's Seeds** – *Eliza Wheeler*
- [ ] **Peep Leap** – *Elizabeth Verdick*
- [ ] **The Tiny Seed** – *Eric Carle*
- [ ] **Sunflower House** – *Eve Bunting*
- [ ] **Jump, Leap, Count Sheep!** – *Geraldo Valério*
- [ ] **Jack's Garden** – *Henry Cole*
- [ ] **Wonders of Nature & the Natural World** – *Jane Werner Watson*
- [ ] **On Duck Pond** – *Jane Yolen*
- [ ] **The Donkey Egg** – *Janet Stevens & Susan Stevens Crummel*
- [ ] **A Tree Is Nice** – *Janice May Udry*
- [ ] **The Busy Tree** – *Jennifer Ward*
- [ ] **Pond** – *Jim LaMarche*
- [ ] **Mr. Gumpy's Outing** – *John Burningham*
- [ ] **Sidewalk Flowers** – *JonArno Lawson*
- [ ] **Fletcher and the Springtime Blossoms** – *Julia Rawlinson*

- [ ] **A Frog in the Bog** – *Karma Wilson*
- [ ] **Over and Under the Pond** – *Kate Messner*
- [ ] **Over and Under the Snow** – *Kate Messner*
- [ ] **Up in the Garden and Down in the Dirt** – *Kate Messner*
- [ ] **My Garden** – *Kevin Henkes*
- [ ] **Waiting** – *Kevin Henkes*
- [ ] **Animal Ark** – *Kwame Alexander*
- [ ] **Frederick** – *Leo Lionni*
- [ ] **Inch by Inch** – *Leo Lionni*
- [ ] **Planting a Rainbow** – *Lois Ehlert*
- [ ] **Red Leaf, Yellow Leaf** – *Lois Ehlert*
- [ ] **Because of an Acorn** – *Lola M. Schaefer & Adam Schaefer*
- [ ] **The Little Island** – *Margaret Wise Brown*
- [ ] **Two Little Gardeners** – *Margaret Wise Brown & Edith Thacher Hurd*
- [ ] **Green Green: A Community Gardening Story** – *Marie Lamba & Baldev Lamba*
- [ ] **The Biggest Puddle in the World** – *Mark Lee*
- [ ] **Wake Up, Island** – *Mary Casanova*
- [ ] **Bringing the Outside In** – *Mary McKenna Siddals*
- [ ] **Carmela Full of Wishes** – *Matt de la Peña*
- [ ] **Sometimes Rain** – *Meg Fleming*
- [ ] **Hello Ocean** – *Pam Muñoz Ryan*
- [ ] **The Wind Blew** – *Pat Hutchins*
- [ ] **The Curious Garden** – *Peter Brown*
- [ ] **Jump, Frog, Jump!** – *Robert Kalan*
- [ ] **Hello, Rock** – *Roger Bradfield*
- [ ] **The Gardener** – *Sarah Stewart*
- [ ] **Hello Lighthouse** – *Sophie Blackall*
- [ ] **Fantastic Flowers** – *Susan Stockdale*
- [ ] **Baby Animals Playing** – *Suzi Eszterhas*
- [ ] **Watersong** – *Tim McCanna*
- [ ] **Daylight Starlight Wildlife** – *Wendell Minor*

Food

- [ ] **Bilal Cooks Daal** – *Aisha Saeed*
- [ ] **No Kimchi For Me!** – *Aram Kim*
- [ ] **Rainbow Stew** – *Cathryn Falwell*
- [ ] **Escargot** – *Dashka Slater*
- [ ] **Pancakes, Pancakes!** – *Eric Carle*
- [ ] **Night of the Veggie Monster** – *George McClements*
- [ ] **Pumpkin Soup** – *Helen Cooper*
- [ ] **Dumpling Soup** – *Jama Kim Rattigan*

- ☐ **Cook-a-Doodle-Doo!** – *Janet Stevens & Susan Stevens Crummel*
- ☐ **The Prince's Breakfast** – *Joanne Oppenheim*
- ☐ **Time for Cranberries** – *Lisl H. Detlefsen*
- ☐ **Jack and the Hungry Giant: Eat Right With MyPlate** – *Loreen Leedy*
- ☐ **How to Make an Apple Pie and See the World** – *Marjorie Priceman*
- ☐ **Gregory, the Terrible Eater** – *Mitchell Sharmat*

"Today a reader, tomorrow a leader."
– MARGARET FULLER

Music & Song

- ☐ **Singing in the Rain** – *Tim Hopgood*
- ☐ **Tubby the Tuba** – *Paul Tripp*
- ☐ **Squeak, Rumble, Whomp! Whomp! Whomp!** – *Wynton Marsalis*
- ☐ **Max Found Two Sticks** – *Brian Pinkney*
- ☐ **One Love** – *Cedella Marley*
- ☐ **88 Instruments** – *Chris Barton*
- ☐ **We're Going on a Lion Hunt** – *David Axtell*
- ☐ **Groovy Joe** – *Eric Litwin*
- ☐ **Olivia Forms a Band** – *Ian Falconer*
- ☐ **Punk Farm** – *Jarrett J. Krosoczka*
- ☐ **Noisy Bug Sing-Along** – *John Himmelman*
- ☐ **Never Play Music & Song Right Next to the Zoo** – *John Lithgow*
- ☐ **This Jazz Man** – *Karen Ehrhardt*
- ☐ **Little Melba and her Big Trombone** – *Katheryn Russell-Brown*
- ☐ **Zin! Zin! Zin! A Violin** – *Lloyd Moss*
- ☐ **Marsh Music** – *Marianne Berkes*
- ☐ **Baby Beluga** – *Raffi*
- ☐ **Los Mariachis** – *Rita Rosa Ruesga*
- ☐ **Trombone Shorty** – *Troy Andrews*
- ☐ **Music, Music & Song for Everyone** – *Vera B. Williams*
- ☐ **Giraffes Can't Dance** – *Giles Andreae*

Seasons

- ☐ **The Reader** – *Amy Hest*
- ☐ **Ten Ways to Hear Snow** – *Cathy Camper*
- ☐ **The Most Perfect Snowman** – *Chris Britt*
- ☐ **Ollie's Ski Trip** – *Elsa Beskow*
- ☐ **Brambly Hedge:Winter Story** – *Jill Barklem*
- ☐ **Big Snow** – *Jonathan Bean*
- ☐ **Red Sled** – *Lita Judge*
- ☐ **Winter Dance** – *Marion Dane Bauer*

- ☐ **Wolf in the Snow** – *Matthew Cordell*
- ☐ **Snowman's Story** – *Will Hillenbrand*
- ☐ **The Winter Visitors** – *Karel Hayes*
- ☐ **Muncha! Muncha! Muncha!** – *Candace Fleming*
- ☐ **Stranger in the Woods** – *Carl R Sams II & Jean Stoick*
- ☐ **The Snowy Nap** – *Jan Brett*
- ☐ **The Three Snow Bears** – *Jan Brett*
- ☐ **Worm Weather** – *Jean Taft*
- ☐ **And Then It's Spring** – *Julie Fogliano*
- ☐ **Goodbye Autumn, Hello Winter** – *Kenard Pak*
- ☐ **Shake a Leg, Egg!** – *Kurt Cyrus*
- ☐ **Stopping by Woods on a Snowy Evening** – *Robert Frost*
- ☐ **Ivy in Bloom: The Poetry of Spring from Great Poets and Writers from the Past** – *Vanita Oelschlager*
- ☐ **Love from the Crayons** – *Drew Daywalt*
- ☐ **If You Take a Mouse to the Movies** – *Laura Numeroff*
- ☐ **Katy and the Big Snow** – *Virginia Lee Burton*
- ☐ **Almost Time** – *Gary D. Schmidt & Elizabeth Stickney*
- ☐ **Snow Globe Wishes** – *Erin Dealey*
- ☐ **Brave Irene** – *William Steig*
- ☐ **Lawrence in the Fall** – *Matthew Farina*
- ☐ **Fletcher and the Falling Leaves** – *Julia Rawlinson*
- ☐ **Goodbye Summer, Hello Autumn** – *Kenard Pak*
- ☐ **Fall Leaves** – *Loretta Holland*
- ☐ **Apples and Robins** – *Lucie Felix*
- ☐ **Mama, Is It Summer Yet?** – *Nikki McClure*
- ☐ **Bunny's First Spring** – *Sally Lloyd-Jones*
- ☐ **Goodbye Winter, Hello Spring** – *Kenard Pak*
- ☐ **Crinkle, Crackle, CRACK: It's Spring!** – *Marion Dane Bauer*
- ☐ **How Many Seeds in a Pumpkin?** – *Margaret McNamara*

- ☐ **Possum and the Summer Storm** – *Anne Hunter*
- ☐ **There Might Be Lobsters** – *Carolyn Crimi*
- ☐ **A Camping Spree with Mr. Magee** – *Chris Van Dusen*
- ☐ **Beach House** – *Deanna Caswell*
- ☐ **At Night** – *Jonathan Bean*
- ☐ **Come On, Rain!** – *Karen Hesse*
- ☐ **Sea Glass Summer** – *Michelle Houts*
- ☐ **My Awesome Summer** – *Paul Meisel*
- ☐ **And Then Comes Summer** – *Tom Brenner*
- ☐ **Summer Days and Nights** – *Wong Herbert Yee*
- ☐ **Tap the Magic Tree** – *Christie Matheson*
- ☐ **The Raft** – *Jim LaMarche*

Sports

- ☐ **Goodnight Hockey Fan** – *Andrew Larsen*
- ☐ **1,2,3, Jump!** – *Lisl Detlefsen*
- ☐ **The Princess and the Pit Stop** – *Tom Angleberger*
- ☐ **The Field** – *Baptiste Paul*
- ☐ **Pepper and Frannie** – *Catherine L. Odell*
- ☐ **Mama Lion Wins the Race** – *Jon Muth*
- ☐ **Randy Riley's Really Big Hit** – *Chris Van Dusen*
- ☐ **Bats at the Ballgame** – *Brian Lies*
- ☐ **Swish!** – *Bill Martin Jr.*
- ☐ **She's Got This!** – *Laurie Hernandez*
- ☐ **Max and Marla** – *Alexandra Boiger*

Why 1000 Books?

[1] http://bit.ly/1000BooksVocab

[2] http://bit.ly/1000BooksBrain

[3] http://bit.ly/1000BooksGrades

[4] http://bit.ly/1000BooksStress

[5] http://bit.ly/1000BooksEmpathy

[6] http://bit.ly/1000BooksWellbeing

[7] http://bit.ly/1000BooksRoleModel

Singing With Books

[1] http://bit.ly/1000BooksSinging

[2] http://bit.ly/1000BooksMovement

Too Many Books

[1] http://bit.ly/1000BooksMontessori

[2] http://bit.ly/1000BooksGiving

Playing With Books

[1] http://bit.ly/1000BooksPlay

Further Reading & Resources

[1] Trelease, J., & Giorgis, C. (2019). *Jim Trelease's Read Aloud Handbook.* Penguin.

[2] Suskind, D. (2015). *Thirty Million Words: Building a Child's Brain.* Dutton.

[3] http://bit.ly/1000BooksResources

[4] http://bit.ly/1000BooksRaisingReaders

[5] http://bit.ly/1000BooksEducators